D1560410

NATIONAL GEOGRAPHIC

Reach™

Language • Literacy • Content

Program Authors

Nancy Frey

Lada Kratky

Nonie K. Lesaux

Sylvia Linan-Thompson

Deborah J. Short

Jennifer D. Turner

NATIONAL GEOGRAPHIC

Hampton-Brown

Literature Reviewers

Carmen Agra Deedy, Grace Lin, Jonda C. McNair, Anastasia Suen

Grade 1 Teacher Reviewers

Kristin Blathras
Lead Literacy Teacher
Donald Morrill Elementary School
Chicago, IL

Anna Ciani
ESL Teacher
PS 291X
Bronx, NY

Jonathan Eversoll
International Baccalaureate Curriculum Coach
Park Center Senior High
Brooklyn Park, MN

Barbara A. Genovese-Fraracci
District Program Specialist
Hacienda La Puente Unified School District
Hacienda Heights, CA

Vanessa Gonzalez
ESL Teacher/ESL Specialist
Rhoads Elementary
Katy, TX

Leonila Izaguirre
Bilingual-ESL Director
Pharr – San Juan – Alamo Independent School District
Pharr, TX

Myra Junyk
Literacy Consultant
Toronto, ON, Canada

Susan Mayberger
Coordinator of ESL, Migrant and Refugee Education
Omaha Public Schools
Omaha, NE

Stephanie Savage Cantu
Bilingual Teacher
Stonewall Jackson Elementary School
Dallas, TX

Annette Torres Elias
Consultant
Plano, TX

Sonia James Upton
ELL Consultant, Title III
Kentucky Department of Education
Frankfort, KY

Acknowledgments

Grateful acknowledgment is given to the authors, artists, photographers, museums, publishers, and agents for permission to reprint copyrighted material. Every effort has been made to secure the appropriate permission. If any omissions have been made or if corrections are required, please contact the Publisher.

Cover Design and Art Direction:
Visual Asylum

Cover Illustration:
Joel Sotelo

Acknowledgments and credits continue on page 295.

The National Geographic Society
John M. Fahey, Jr., President & Chief Executive Officer
Gilbert M. Grosvenor, Chairman of the Board

National Geographic School Publishing
Hampton-Brown
www.NGSP.com

Printed in the USA.
RR Donnelley, Jefferson City, MO

ISBN: 978-0-7362-7426-5

ISBN (TX): 978-0-7362-7490-6

11 12 13 14 15 16 17 18 19

10 9 8 7 6 5 4

Contents at a Glance

Unit 5

Creature Features

BIG QUESTION

How are animals different?

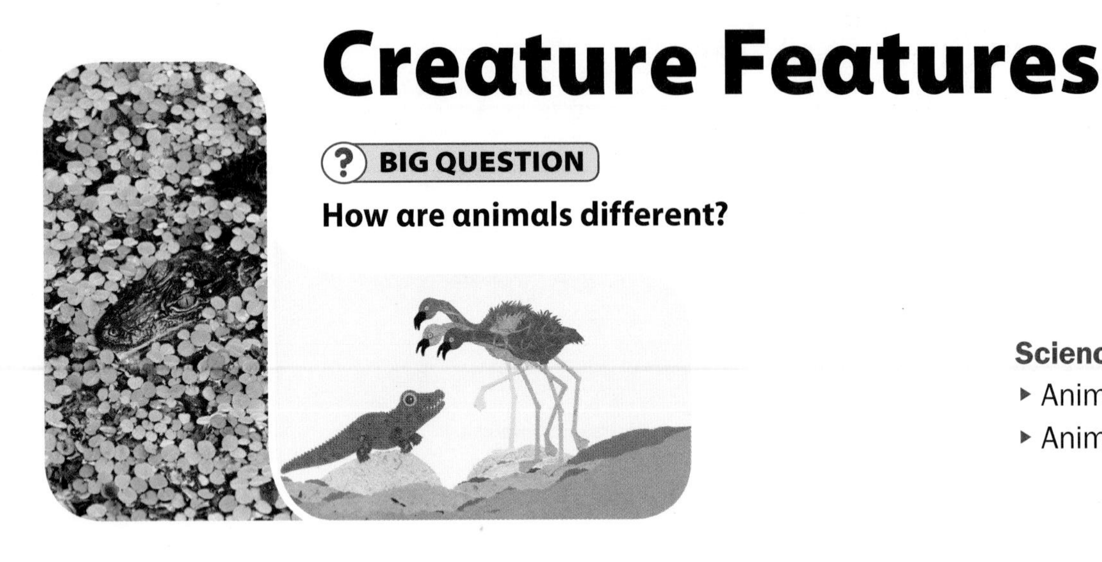

Science
- Animal Features
- Animal Movement

NGReach.com Sing-with-Me MP3s ▪ Read-with-Me MP3s ▪ National Geographic Digital Library ▪ Interactive eEdition ▪ Games for learning ▪ My Vocabulary Notebook ▪ Online Resources

Up in the Air

BIG QUESTION

What's wild about weather?

Science
- Weather
- Seasons

NGReach.com
Sing-with-Me MP3s ▪ Read-with-Me MP3s ▪ National Geographic Digital Library ▪ Interactive eEdition ▪ Games for learning ▪ My Vocabulary Notebook ▪ Online Resources

Unit 7

Then and Now

What's the difference between then and now?

Social Studies
- Past and Present
- Inventions and Technology

NGReach.com Sing-with-Me MP3s (MP3) ▪ Read-with-Me MP3s (MP3) ▪ National Geographic Digital Library ▪ Interactive eEdition ▪ Games for learning ▪ My Vocabulary Notebook ▪ Online Resources

Get Out the Map!

BIG QUESTION

Why do we need maps?

Social Studies
- Maps
- Signs and Symbols

NGReach.com Sing-with-Me MP3s (MP3) ▪ Read-with-Me MP3s (MP3) ▪ National Geographic Digital Library ▪ Interactive eEdition ▪ Games for learning ▪ My Vocabulary Notebook ▪ Online Resources

Genres at a Glance

Fiction

Animal Fantasy

Legend

Modern Fairy Tale

Realistic Fiction

Poetry

Haiku

Poem

Nonfiction

Media

Creature Features

BIG Question How are animals different?

Unit at a Glance

- **Language**: Compare and Contrast, Give Information, Science Words
- **Literacy**: Make Connections
- **Content**: Animals

Unit 5

Share What You Know

Do It!

1. **Draw** an animal.
2. **Name** or point to different parts of your animal.
3. **Say** or show how your animal moves.

Build background: Watch a video about animals.
NGReach.com

High Frequency Words
and
but
too

Compare and Contrast

Listen and chant.

Legs

Chant MP3

Flamingos have legs,
And alligators do, **too**.
Alligators have four legs,
But flamingos have two!

Key Words

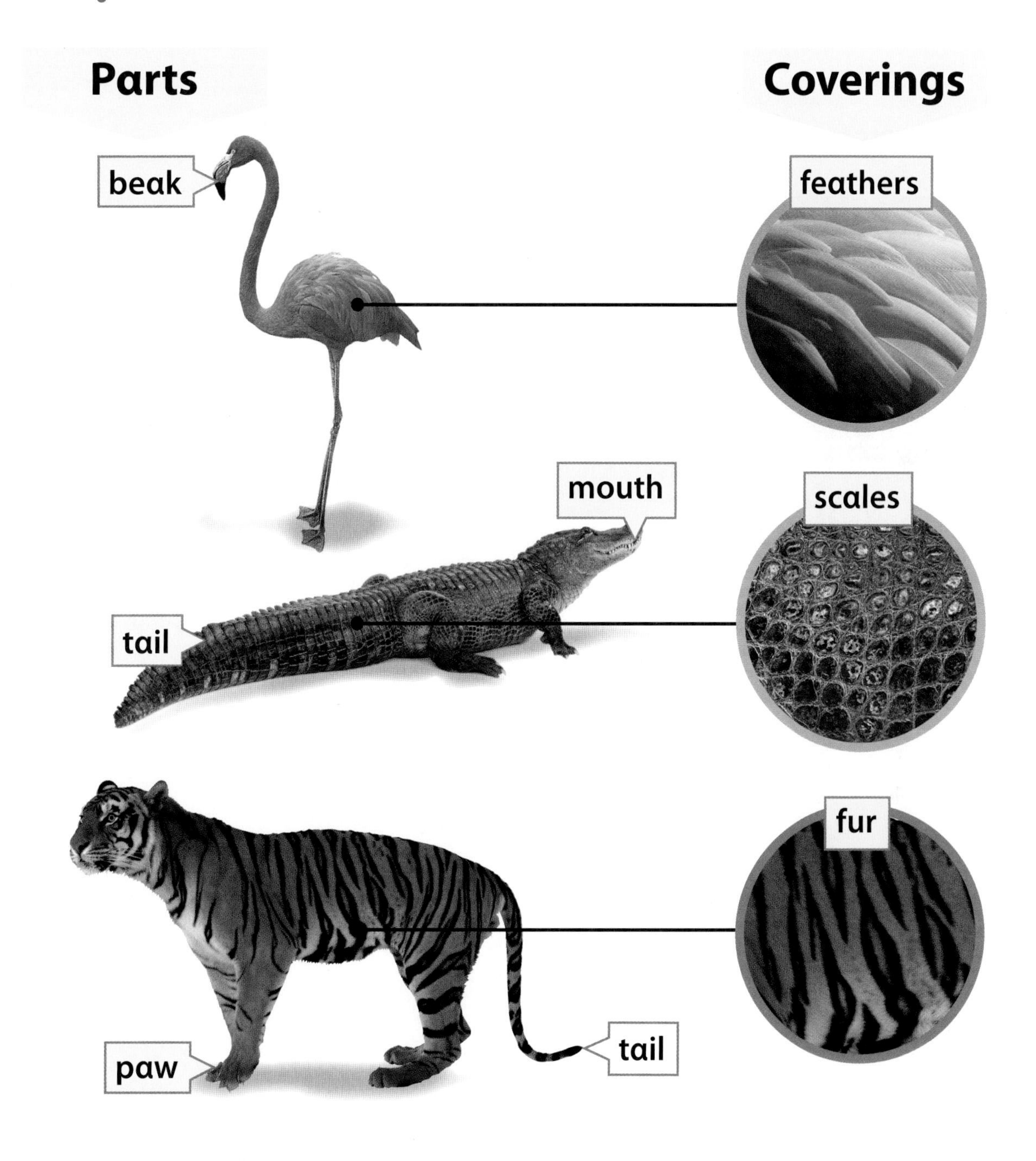

Talk Together

Look at the parts and coverings of animals on this page. How are they different?

Compare and Contrast

Venn Diagram

To compare, write what is the same here.

alligator
- scales
- tail

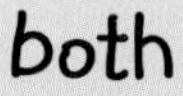

both
- legs

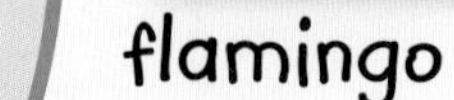

flamingo
- feathers
- beak

To contrast, write what is different here.

Talk Together

Choose two animal picture cards. Make a Venn diagram. Compare and contrast the animals.

More Key Words

alike

These cats are **alike**.

• body

A baby has a small **body**.

different

These fruits are **different**.

feature

A long neck is the main **feature** of a giraffe.

• look

These apples **look** the same.

Talk Together

Use one **Key Word** in a sentence.

I look like my brother.

Add words to My Vocabulary Notebook.

NGReach.com

• High Frequency Word

Read a Story

An **animal fantasy** is a story that is not true. The animals act like people.

Characters

Characters are the people or animals in the story.

Pete

Pete's Friends

Reading Strategy

Make connections as you read.

How are your feelings like Pete's feelings?

For Pete's Sake

by **Ellen Stoll Walsh**

“I’m green,” said Pete. “I want to be pink. Everyone else is.”

"Don't worry," said the others. "You probably aren't ripe yet. It takes longer for some."

“Is that true?” Pete wondered.

“Probably,” they said. “Let’s play in the sand!”

“Oh no,” cried Pete. “I have four feet. No one else has four feet.”

"You're lucky, Pete," said the others. "Two, and two extra. C'mon. Let's go wading."

Pete tried to feel lucky.

Before long he was having fun.

“Stop!” said the others, laughing.
“You’re getting our **feathers** wet.”
Uh-oh. Pete didn’t have any feathers.

"The best feathers take the longest to grow," they said. "Hurry, it's getting late."

The others hurried home.

But poor, green, featherless Pete poked along on his four feet…

very, very slowly.

Nothing could cheer him up.

Then one day some strangers stopped by on their way to the swamp. Flamingos who **looked** just like Pete.

Pete almost popped with joy.

"I'm **different** but the same," he told the others.

"Well, for Pete's sake, Pete," they said. "You always have been." ❖

AWARD WINNER

Meet the Author

Ellen Stoll Walsh

Ellen Stoll Walsh has nine brothers and sisters. Ellen was the family storyteller.

Ellen grew up and started writing stories to read to her children. Now she can't imagine doing anything else!

Writer's Craft

Find words that Ellen Stoll Walsh used to show what Pete and his friends look like. Can you add some words?

Talk About It

1. What do Pete and his friends do together?

   Pete and his friends ____ .

2. What does Pete want? Why?

   Pete wants ____ . He ____ .

3. Do you think Pete's friends like him the way he is? Explain.

   I think Pete's friends ____ .

Learn test-taking strategies.
NGReach.com

Write About It

Make connections. How are your friends like Pete's friends? How are they **different**?

Pete's friends ____ and my friends are ____ .
Pete's friends ____ but my friends are ____ .

Compare Characters

How are the characters different?

How are they **alike**?

Venn Diagram

Pete	both	Pete's friends
• green •	• like to play	• •

Use your diagram. Tell a partner about Pete and Pete's friends.

Pete's friends have feathers.

Synonyms

alike	same
The flamingos are **alike**.	The flamingos are the **same**.

Alike and **same** are **synonyms**. They have the same meaning.

Try It Together

Talk about these pairs of words. Are they synonyms? Why or why not?

object	thing
sick	happy
bad	paw
quickly	fast

Connect Across Texts Learn more about what makes alligators **different**.

Genre A **science article** is nonfiction. This article gives information about alligators.

ALLIGATORS

by Julie Larson

An Alligator Home

Many alligators live in the Florida Everglades. The Everglades has many rivers and islands.

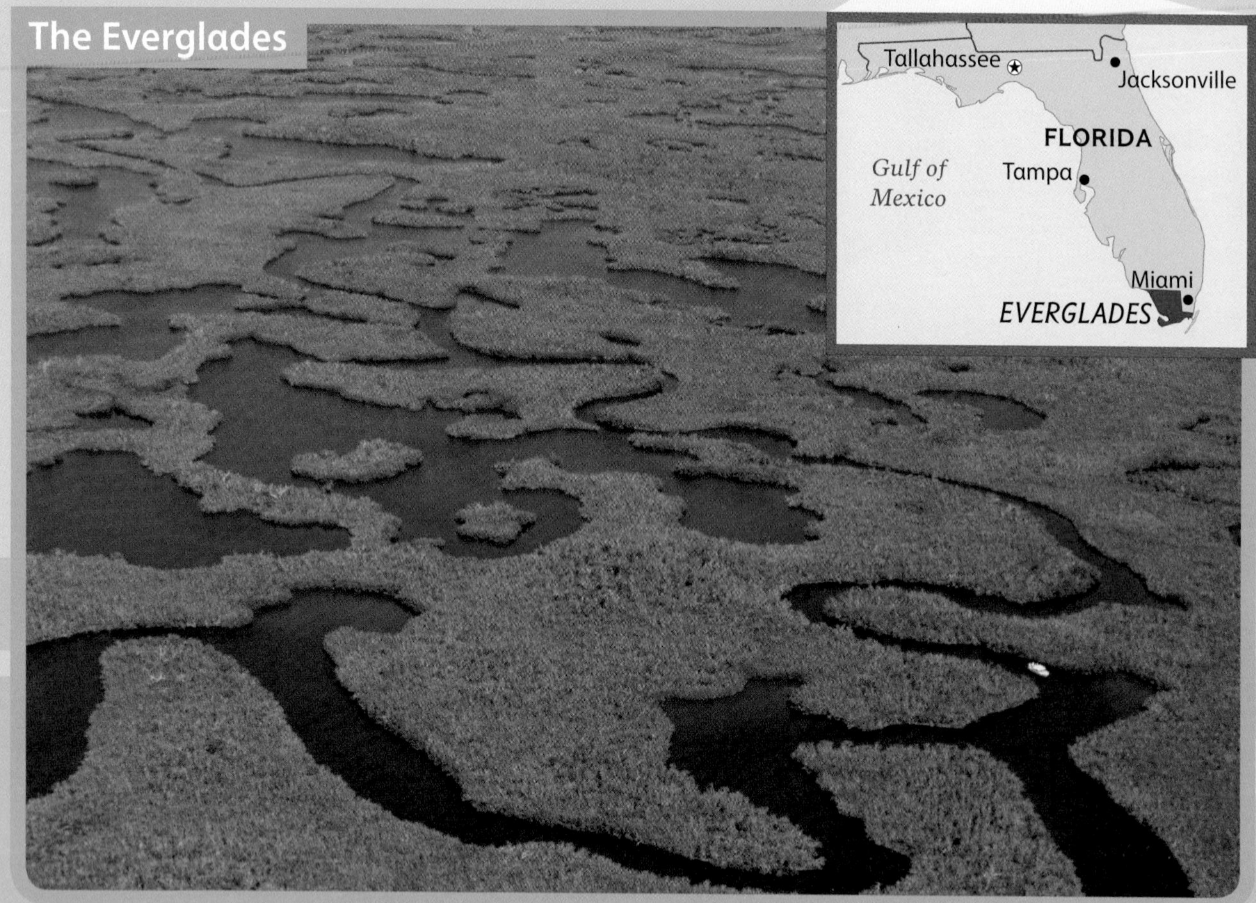
The Everglades

How do alligators' **bodies** help them live in the Everglades? Let's find out.

Alligator Bodies

Alligators have short legs. They can hide in tall grass. They can also hide under the water. Sometimes, you can only see their eyes. Can you see the alligator?

Alligator Tails

Alligator **tails** can be more than 5 feet long. This is probably taller than you! Tails help alligators swim and move through the mud.

Tails help alligators leap up to catch food. Alligators can leap 5 feet into the air!

Compare Genres

How are *For Pete's Sake* and "Alligators" different?

Animal Fantasy

Then one day some strangers stopped by on their way to the swamp. Flamingos who looked just like Pete.
Pete almost popped with joy.
Animals have feelings.
26

Science Article

Alligator Bodies
Alligators have short legs. They can hide in tall grass. They can also hide under the water. Sometimes, you can only see their eyes. Can you see the alligator?
gives information

Talk Together

Think about what you read and learned. How are animals different?

Complete Sentences

A **sentence** tells a complete thought.

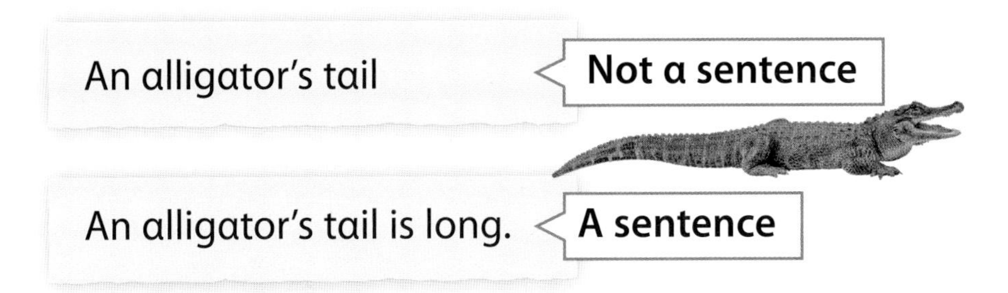

An alligator's tail
Not a sentence
An alligator's tail is long.
A sentence

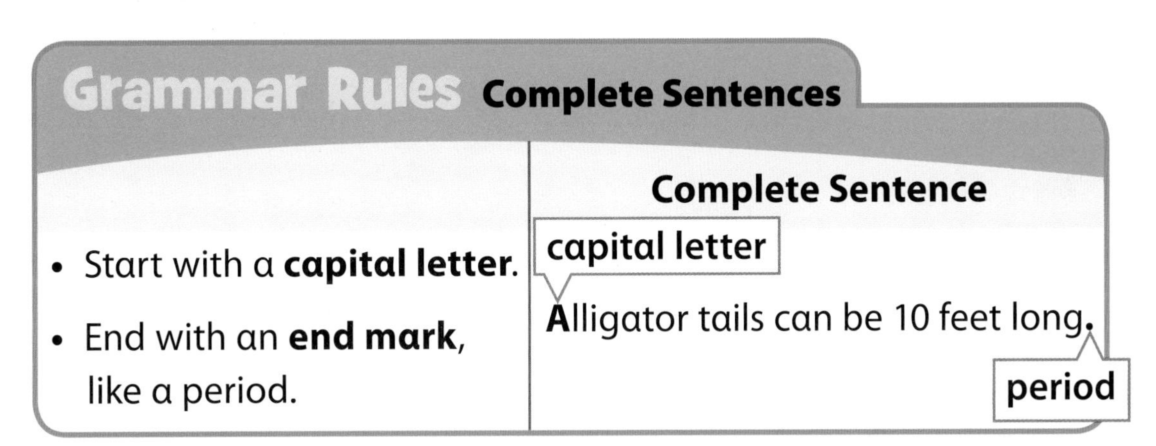

Grammar Rules **Complete Sentences**

	Complete Sentence
• Start with a **capital letter**. • End with an **end mark**, like a period.	capital letter **A**lligator tails can be 10 feet long**.** period

Read a Sentence

Which group of words is a sentence?

How do you know?

1. leap up
2. Tails help alligators leap up to catch food.

Write a Sentence 

Write a sentence about alligators. Read it to a partner.

High Frequency Words
is
this
use

Give Information

Listen and chant.

Chant ((MP3))

How Do They Move?

Animals move.
Yes, they do.
How do they go?
Do you know?

This is a fish.
A fish swims.
A fish uses fins to
move in water!

Fish swim.
Yes, they do.
How do they go?
Now you know!

Key Words

How do animals move?

swim

A fish swims.

fly

A bird flies.

run

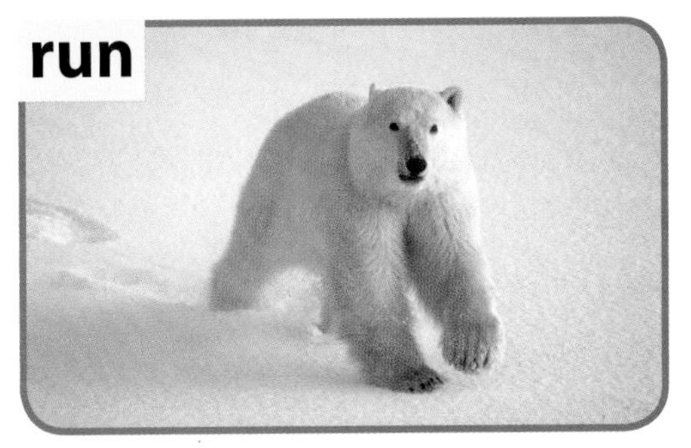

A polar bear runs.

climb

A monkey climbs.

slide

A penguin slides.

slither

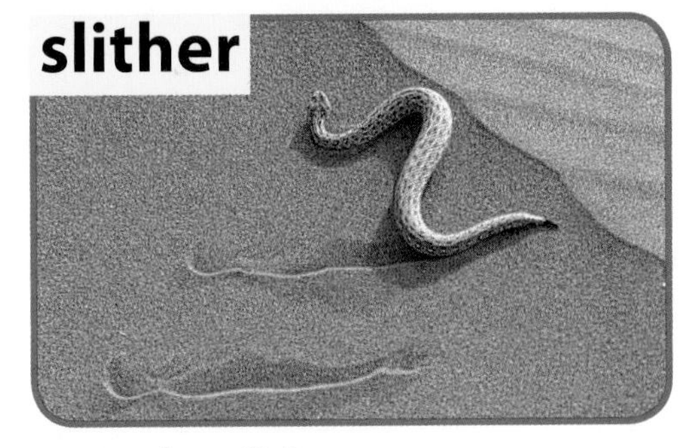

A snake slithers.

Talk Together

Act out how animals move. How are animals different?

Categorize Details

Category Chart

Animals	Movement
fish turtle	swim
	fly
	run

Write the big ideas here.

Write the details here.

Talk Together

Sort picture cards. Add animals to the Category Chart. Act out how the animals move. How are they different?

More Key Words

• **back**	**fact**	**front**

The **back** tire is flat.	It's a **fact** that a dog has four legs.	The **front** of the house is blue.

movement	**push**

The **movement** of a turtle is slow.	We had to **push** the car.

• High Frequency Word

Talk Together

Use a **Key Word** to ask a question about animals.

What is one fact about turtles?

Add words to My Vocabulary Notebook.

NGReach.com

Read a Fact Book

A **fact book** is nonfiction. It gives facts about things that are real.

✓ Look for labels.

Reading Strategy

Make connections as you read. Connect new facts to things you have read in other texts and to things you know about the world.

Slither, Slide, Hop, and Run

by Katharine Kenah

Comprehension Coach

A bird can **fly**! It moves through the air with wings.

Slither

A snake can **slither**! It wiggles from side to side on the ground.

Hop

A kangaroo can hop! It makes short leaps into the air. It uses its **back** feet to hop.

Run

A horse can **run**! Its legs move forward and backward very quickly.

Slide

A snail can **slide**! It moves slowly along the ground. A snail has a soft body inside its hard shell.

Crawl

A spider can crawl! It creeps forward with its legs.

Hang

A sloth can hang! It holds onto a tree and hangs below it. A sloth has long claws.

Swim

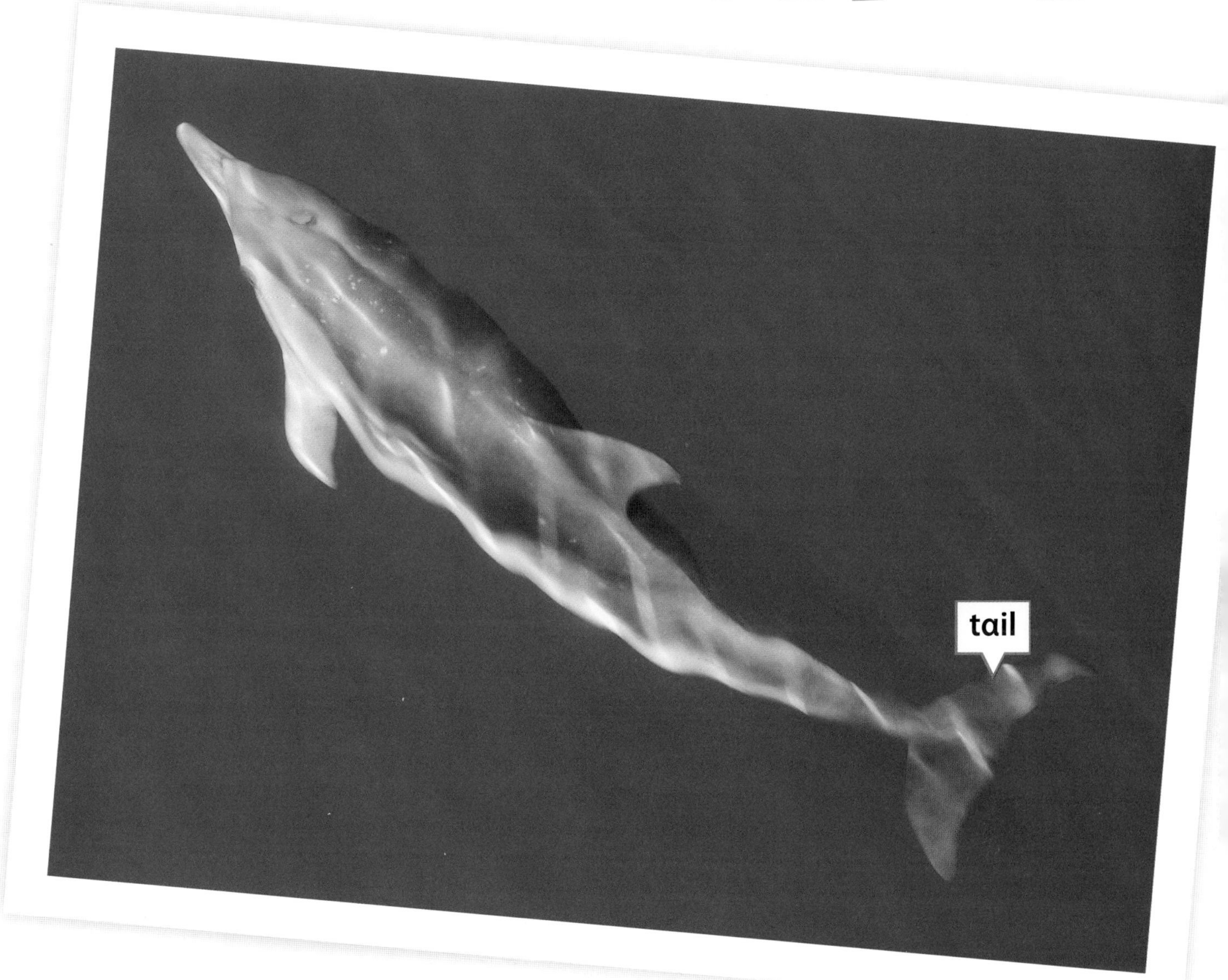

A dolphin can **swim**! It moves gently through the water. A dolphin swims by moving its tail up and down.

Glide

A bat can glide! It flies smoothly through the air. A bat's wings are really long fingers covered with skin.

Dig

A dog can dig! It uses its paws to move dirt.

Climb

A raccoon can **climb**! It moves up and down by using its feet. Its **front** and back feet work like hands.

Waddle

A penguin can waddle! It rocks from side to side as it walks. A penguin can waddle as fast as a person walks!

Talk About It 

1. What does the **fact** book tell you about animals?

   The fact book tells ____ .

2. Choose an animal from the fact book. Explain how it moves.

   A ____ uses its ____ to ____ .

3. How do other books you have read help you understand this fact book?

   Other books help me ____ .

Learn test-taking strategies.
NGReach.com

Write About It 

What is interesting about how animals move? Write one sentence.

It is interesting that ____ .

Categorize Details

How do animals move?

Category Chart

Animals	Movement
birds bats	fly
horses	

Use your chart to summarize what you learned in *Slither, Slide, Hop, and Run.*

Antonyms

big	small
The horse is **big**.	The snail is **small**.

Big and **small** have opposite meanings. Words with opposite meanings are called **antonyms**.

Try It Together

Choose animal picture cards. Use the antonyms to compare the animals.

Antonyms	
big	small
fast	slow
front	back
hard	soft

Connect Across Texts Read about a camera that films animals moving in different ways.

Genre A **photo journal** shows something important in a person's life. It uses words and photos.

My Crittercam Journal

by Greg Marshall

July 8

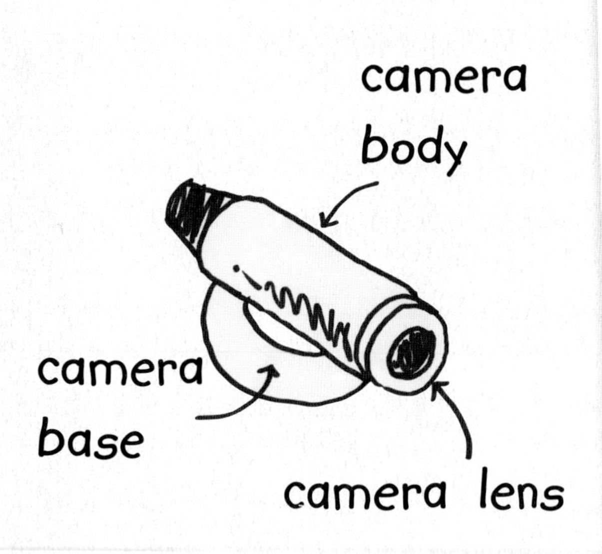

Here's the camera my team and I made. I call it Crittercam.

July 10

Today we put Crittercam on a whale. I saw how it eats and swims.

August 20

I'm in Africa! Today Crittercam filmed a lion's movements. It runs fast!

August 21

Today I watched my Crittercam videos. The penguin video was really exciting.

Compare Genres

How are *Slither, Slide, Hop, and Run* and "My Crittercam Journal" alike and different?

Fact Book

Photo Journal

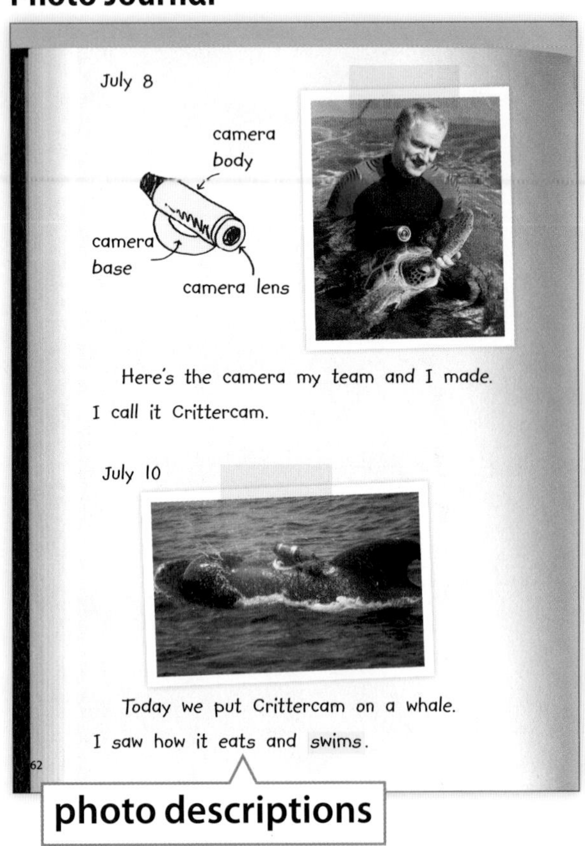

Talk Together

Think about what you read and learned. How are animals different?

Subject-Verb Agreement

In a sentence, the **subject** and the **verb** go together.

One **frog** **hops**.

Two **frogs** **hop**.

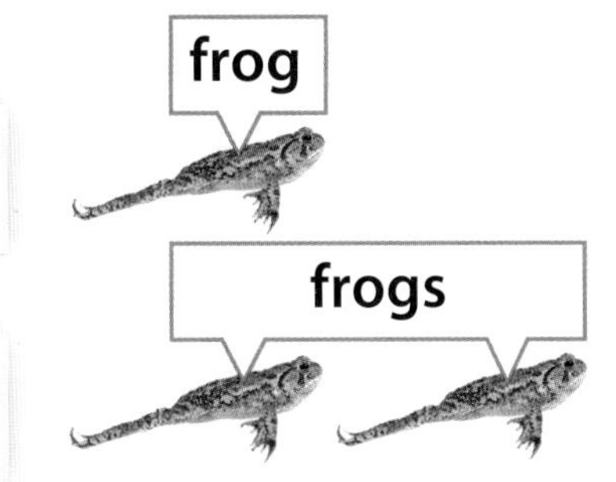

Grammar Rules Subject-Verb Agreement

	Subject-Verb Agreement
If the **subject** names one, use **s** at the end of the **verb**.	If the **subject** names more than one, do not use **s** at the end of the **verb**.

Read a Sentence

Why does the verb below have **s**?

A dolphin **swims** in the ocean.

Write a Sentence

Write a sentence about how an animal moves.

Read it to a partner.

Write Like a Scientist

Write an Article

What do you know about animals? Describe an animal. Write an article for your classmates.

Penguins

by Roberto Garcia

main idea > **A penguin is a special bird**. Most birds have wings. Most birds use their wings to fly.

details > **A penguin has wings. But it doesn't fly**! Penguins use their wings to swim under water.

An article gives information about a topic.

Language Frames

- The main idea of my article is ____ .

❶ Plan and Write

Talk about animals with a partner. Pick an animal. Discuss your plan. Draw your animal and write a list of details. Tell your partner your main idea.

Write your main idea. Then write sentences with details.

❷ Check Your Work

Revise and edit your writing. Use this checklist.

Checklist

- ☑ Think about different words you can use. Can you use synonyms?
- ☑ Check your sentences. Did you use the right end mark?
- ☑ Trade work with a partner. Check the spelling. Correct spelling errors.

❸ Finish and Share

Finish your drawing. Write each sentence neatly. Make sure you leave enough space between each sentence.

Read your article aloud. Listen to your partner's article. Share what you know.

I know that peguins can't fly.

BIG Question
How are animals different?

Share Your Ideas

Think about how animals move and look. How are animals different? Choose one of these ways to share your ideas about the **Big Question**.

Write It!

tail
legs
teeth
Alligators have four legs.

Draw and Label

Draw your favorite animal from the unit. Label the animal's parts. Write a sentence about your animal.

Talk About It!

Interview

Have an interview with a partner. The **reporter** asks questions about how animals look and move. The **expert** answers the questions.

How do penguins move?

Reporter

They waddle!

Expert

Do It!

I Am an Animal

Pretend you are an animal. Make a mask. In a group, act out how your animal moves.

Up in the Air

BIG Question

What's wild about weather?

Unit at a Glance

- **Language**: Explain, Express Ideas, Science Words
- **Literacy**: Make Inferences
- **Content**: Weather

Unit 6

Share What You Know

Do It!

1. **Name** your favorite kind of weather.
2. **Tell** why you like that weather.
3. **Draw** something you do in that weather.

Build Background: Watch a video about weather.

NGReach.com

High Frequency Words
can
how
made

Explain

Listen and sing.

Song MP3

Wind

The wind is made of air.
The wind is made of air.
Let me explain it one more time
How wind is made of air.

Wind can blow trees down.
And blow your hat around.
Let me explain it one more time
How wind can blow trees down.

Tune: "The Farmer in the Dell"

Key Words

What happens when the **wind blows**?

Weather changes.

It can make electricity.

Things move.

It **feels** good.

Talk Together

Look at the windy weather. Explain what different kinds of wind can do. What is wild about wind?

Find Cause and Effect

Cause-and-Effect Chart

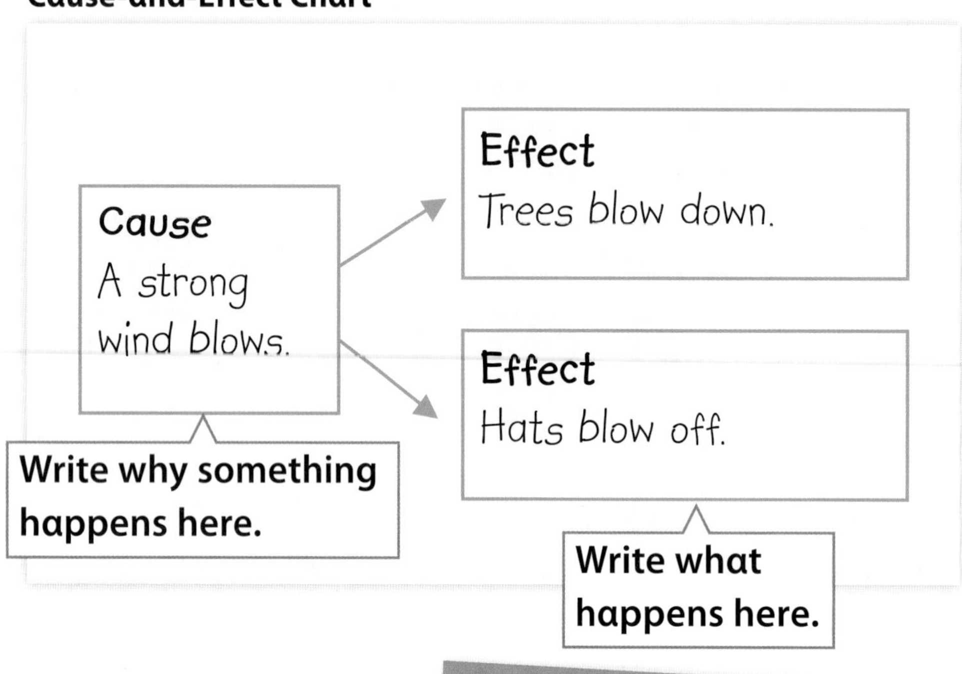
Cause
A strong wind blows.
Effect
Trees blow down.
Effect
Hats blow off.
Write why something happens here.
Write what happens here.

Talk Together

Talk to a partner about rain. Explain what happens when it rains. Make a cause-and-effect chart.

More Key Words

• fast

This car drives **fast**.

outside

They walk **outside**.

power

This toaster uses **power**.

soft

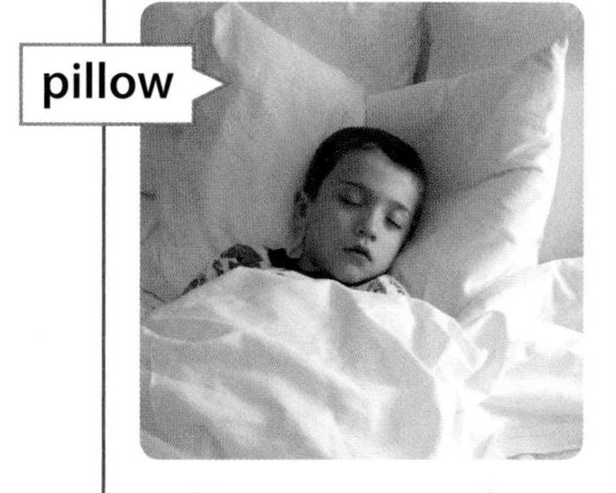

Pillows are **soft**.

strong

We are **strong**.

• High Frequency Word

Talk Together

Sort the **Key Words** by syllables.

One syllable fast

Two syllables outside

Add words to My Vocabulary Notebook.

NGReach.com

Read Science Nonfiction

Science nonfiction gives information about a science topic, like weather.

✓ Look for illustrations. Illustrations are drawings that show information.

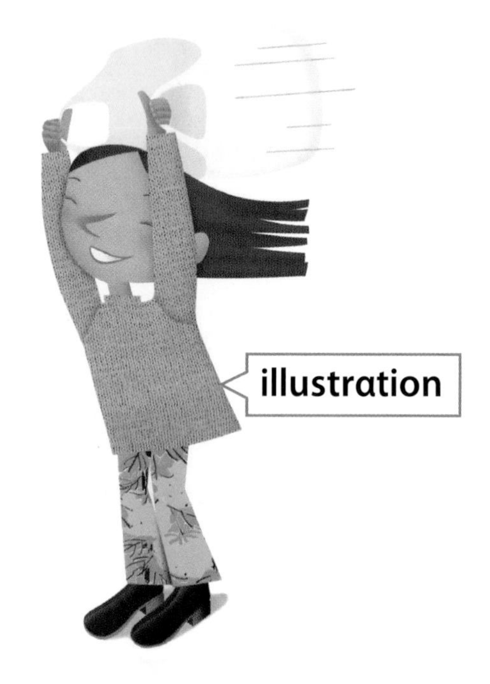

Reading Strategy

Make inferences as you read. Use what you know and details from the text to make inferences about what wind does.

I Face the Wind

by **Vicki Cobb**

illustrated by **Julia Gorton**

Comprehension Coach

Have you ever felt a **strong wind**?

Your hair **blows** away from your face. You could lose your hat. You may even have to walk at a slant.

You can't see the wind. But you can **feel** it. And you can see what wind does to other things.

It makes flags stick out
straight and flutter.

Can you name some things
you see wind do?

Go **outside** and watch.

Leaves on trees shake.

A kite stays in the sky.

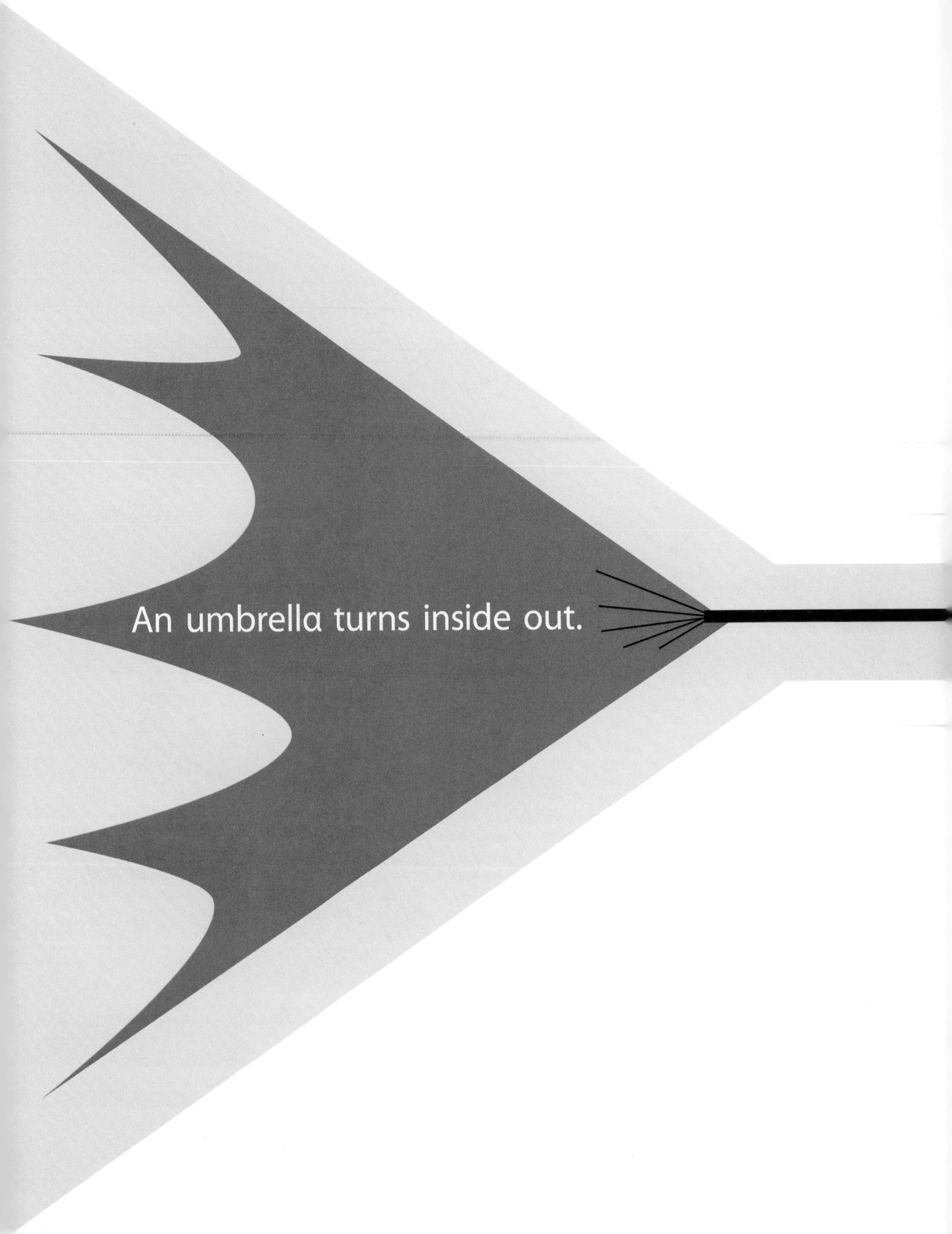

An umbrella turns inside out.

What is wind made of?

Wind is made of air. You can't see air. But you can catch it. Here's how:

1. Open a large plastic bag. Make sure there are no holes in it.
2. Pull the bag through the air so it puffs up.

3. Twist it closed to trap the air you caught.

4. Squeeze the bag to feel the air.

Are there other ways you can make wind?

Blow air out of your mouth. Wave your hand in front of your face. Be an inventor and make your own kind of air movers.

The **fastest** winds of all are in a tornado. These winds are so strong they can lift a roof right off a house!

One of the **softest** winds is your breath. Put your fingertips near your nose. Feel your soft breath.

Face the wind. Feel the push of the wind. Yay! ❖

Talk About It 

1. What is **wind** made of?

   Wind is made of ______.

2. What happens when the wind **blows**?

   When the wind blows, ______ will ______.

3. Why might you have to walk at a slant when a **strong** wind blows?

   You might have to walk at a slant because ______.

Learn test-taking strategies.
NGReach.com

Write About It 

Use the illustrations and steps on pages 86 and 87. Retell how to catch air.

You can catch air ______.

Find Cause and Effect

The wind blows. This is the cause.

What are the effects?

Cause-and-Effect Chart

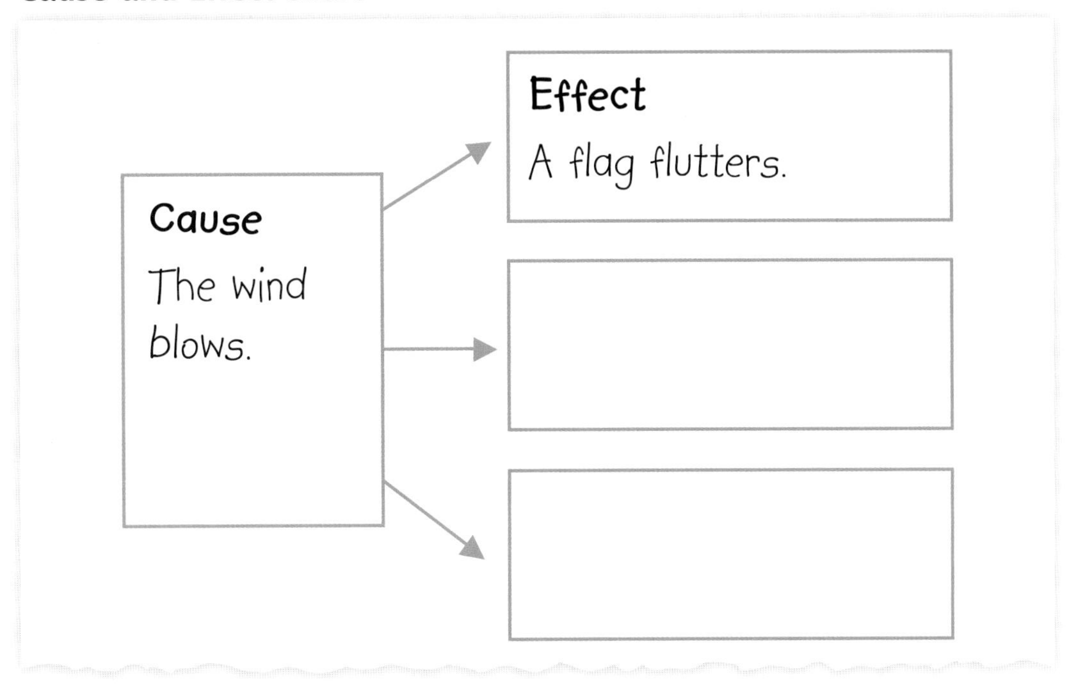

Use your cause-and-effect chart. Tell a partner facts you learned in *I Face the Wind*.

Compound Words

Touch your nose with your fingertips.

finger + tips = fingertips ← compound word

Learn the meanings of both words to understand the **compound word**.

finger	• We have five **fingers** on each hand.
+ tips	• **Tips** mean ends.
fingertips	• **Fingertips** are the ends of fingers.

Try It Together

Talk about the meaning of each compound word.

rain	+	coat	=	raincoat
sun	+	glasses	=	sunglasses
snow	+	man	=	snowman

Use the two shorter words to help you. Then draw a picture to show the compound word. Label your drawing.

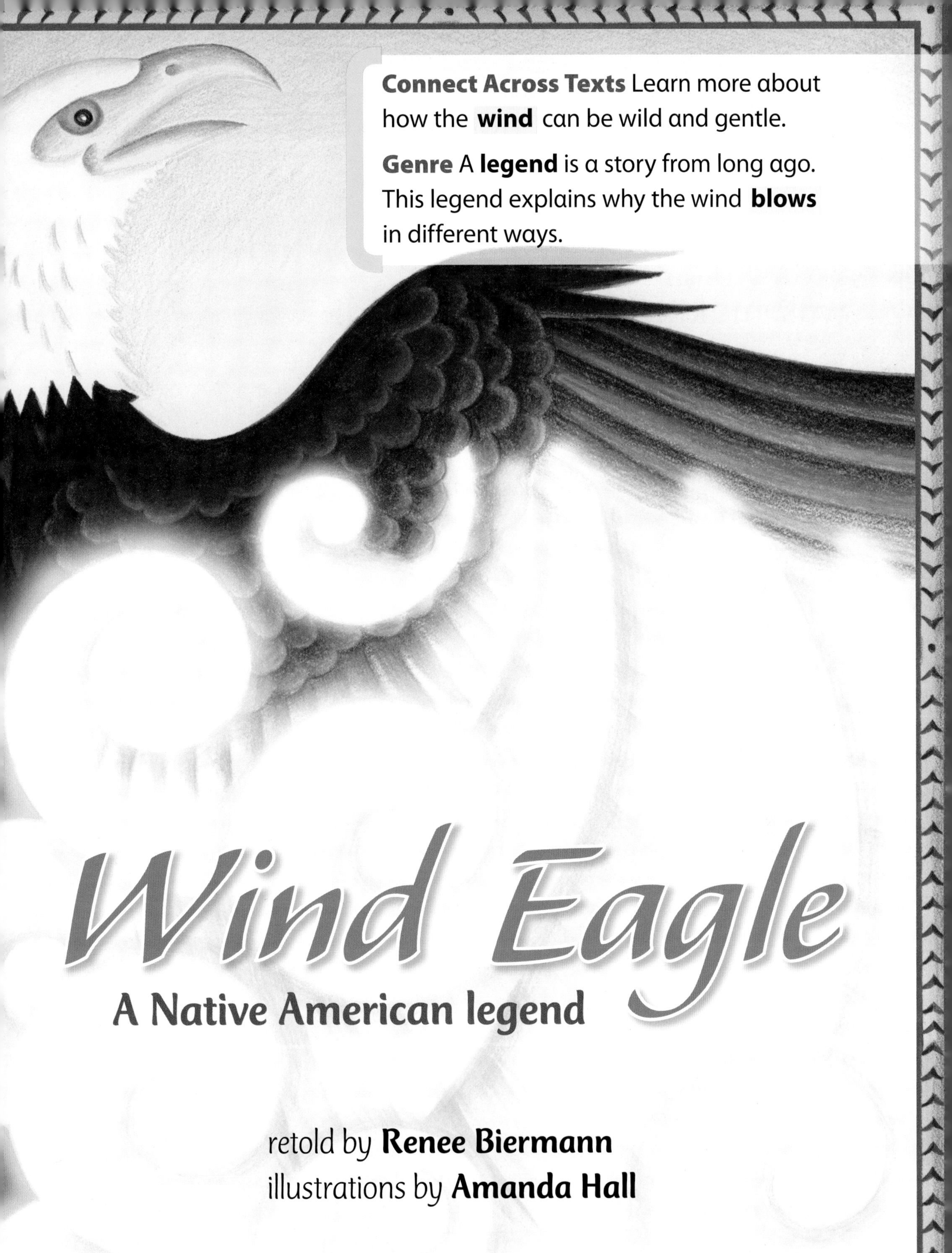

Connect Across Texts Learn more about how the **wind** can be wild and gentle.

Genre A **legend** is a story from long ago. This legend explains why the wind **blows** in different ways.

Wind Eagle

A Native American legend

retold by **Renee Biermann**
illustrations by **Amanda Hall**

Gluscabi could not fish. There was too much wind. The wind pushed his boat. He went to see Wind Eagle. Wind Eagle was making too much wind!

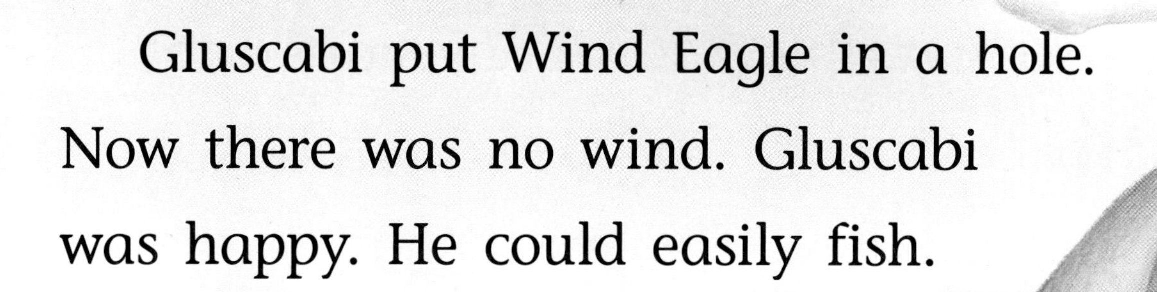

Gluscabi put Wind Eagle in a hole. Now there was no wind. Gluscabi was happy. He could easily fish.

Weeks went by. Bad things started to happen because the wind did not blow. Everyone was hot. The fish began to die. The people in the village were not happy.

Gluscabi went to see Wind Eagle. Wind Eagle promised to make gentle winds. So Gluscabi took Wind Eagle out of the hole.

But on some days Wind Eagle forgets his promise. That's why some days **feel** very windy. ❖

Character's Action

In *Wind Eagle*, what are the reasons for Gluscabi's actions?

Gluscabi's Actions	Reasons
Gluscabi went to see Wind Eagle.	There was too much wind. Gluscabi couldn't fish.
Gluscabi put Wind Eagle in a hole.	
Gluscabi went to see Wind Eagle again.	
Gluscabi took Wind Eagle out of the hole.	

Talk Together

Think about what you read and learned. What's wild about **weather**?

Sentence Types

There are four **types of sentences.**

Grammar Rules Sentence Types

1. A **statement** tells something. It ends with a **period**.	• Gluscabi could not fish. (**period**)
2. A **question** asks something. It ends with an **question mark**.	• Can you feel the wind? (**question mark**)
3. An **exclamation** shows strong feeling. It ends with an **exclamation point**.	• There is too much wind! (**exclamation point**)
4. A **command** tells someone to do something. It starts with a verb. It ends with a **period** or an **exclamation point**.	• Stop, Wind Eagle! (**exclamation point**)

Read a Sentence

What types of sentences are these? How do you know?

It was so hot!

The fish began to die.

Write a Sentence

Write a sentence about today's weather. Read it aloud.

High Frequency Words
see
that
think

Express Ideas

Listen and sing.

Watching the Weather

Song MP3

I **see** big, dark clouds today.

I **think that** we will get rain.

I see a bright sun outside.

I think we'll be hot tonight!

I see snow fall from the sky.

I think we'll have a snowball fight!

Tune: "Twinkle Twinkle, Little Star"

Key Words

What is the weather?

The weather is different every **month** of the **year**.

Talk Together

What is the weather like today? Is it wild?

Classify Details

Classification Chart

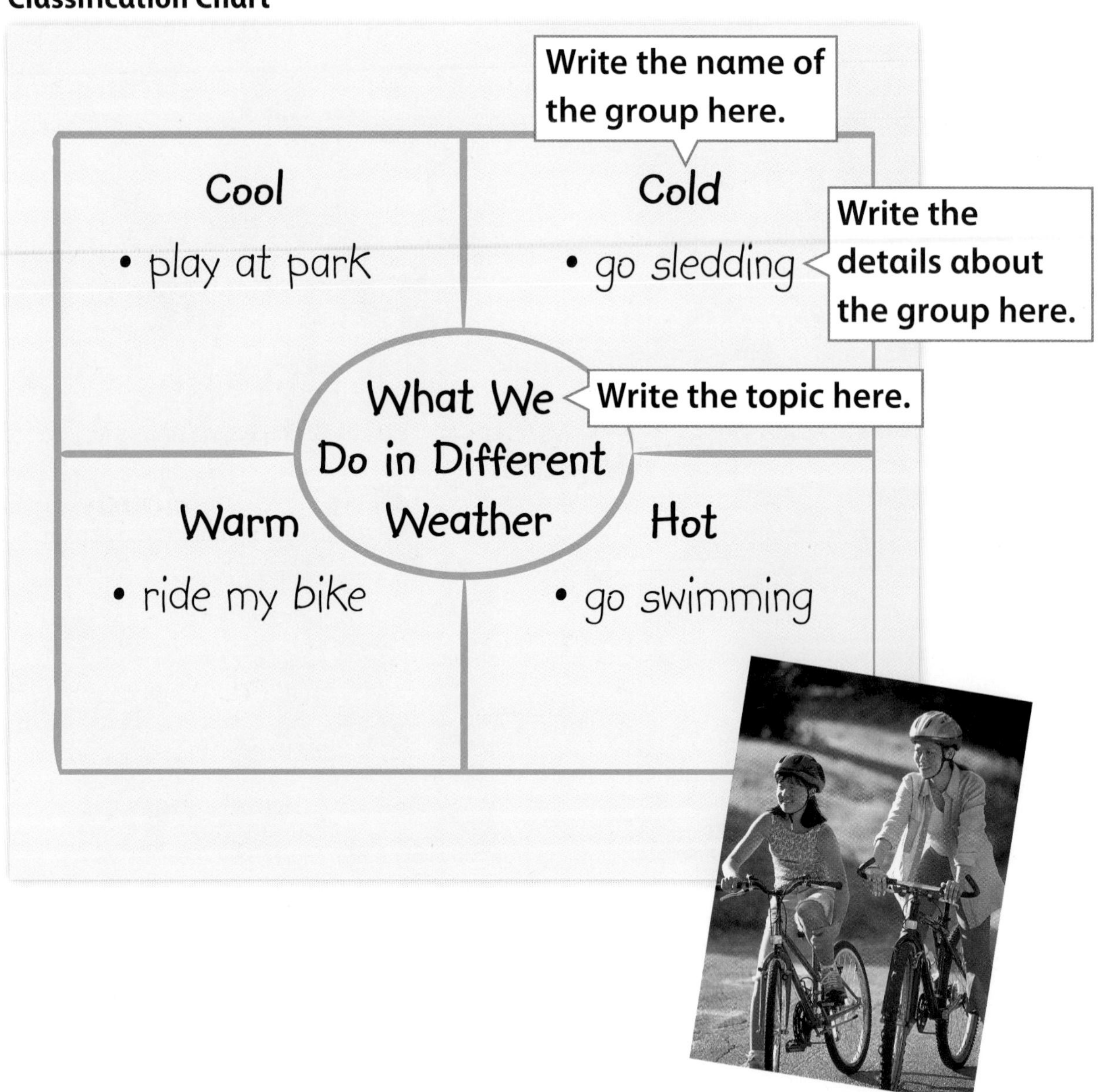

Talk Together

Tell your partner what you do in different kinds of weather. Add to the classification chart. How is your weather wild?

More Key Words

cold

It's **cold** today.

cool

The fan keeps me **cool**.

hot

The stove is **hot**.

temperature

The **temperature** is 8° Fahrenheit.

warm

The blanket keeps us **warm**.

Talk Together

Ask a question using a **Key Word**.

What do you wear when it is cold outside?

Add words to My Vocabulary Notebook.

NGReach.com

Read Realistic Fiction

Realistic fiction is a story that is made up, but could happen in real life.

Sensory Details

Sensory details tell what characters see, hear, smell, taste, and touch.

sensory detail
February is cold and still.

Reading Strategy

Make inferences as you read.

How do you think Kiko feels about the different weather?

A Year for Kiko

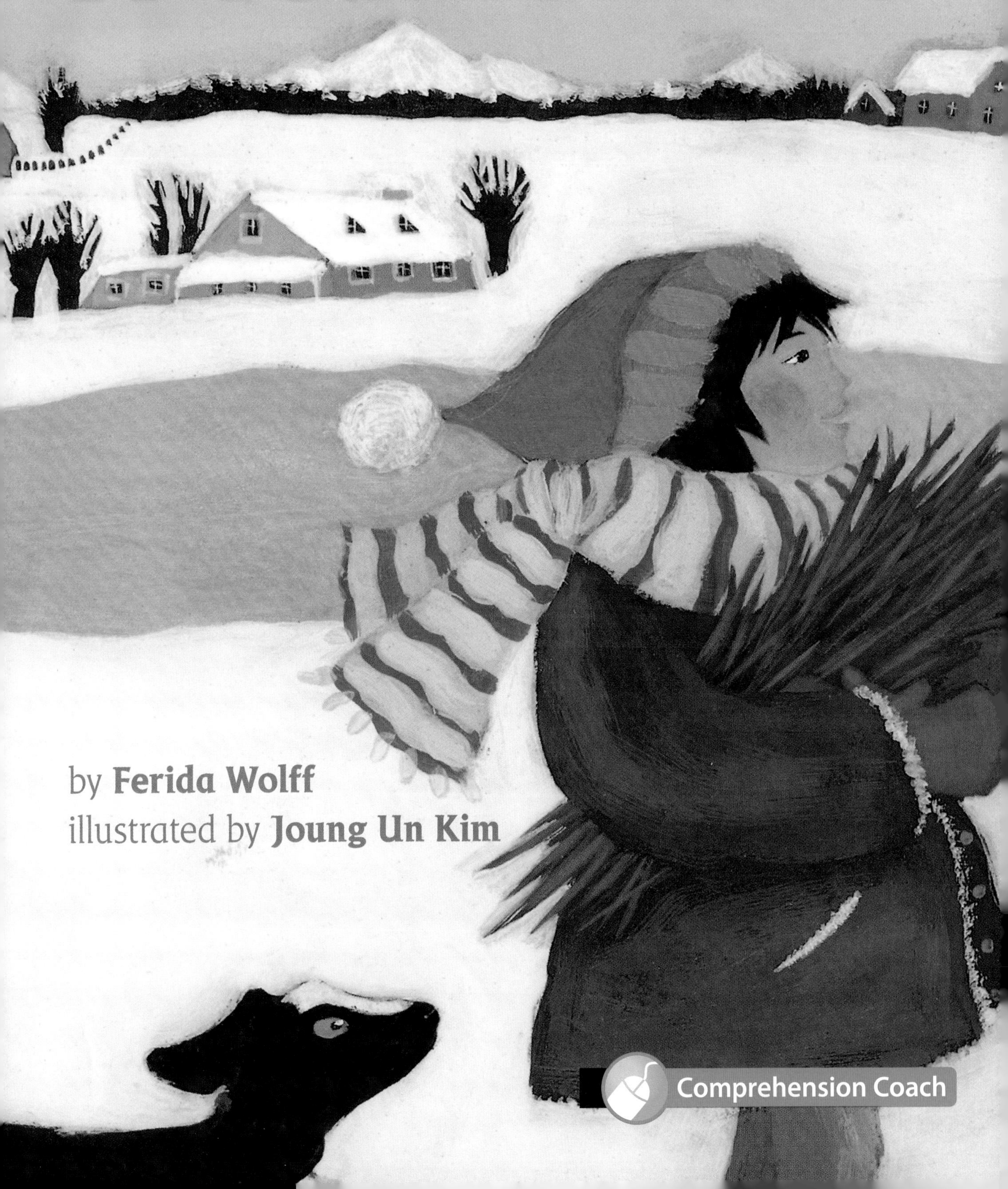

by **Ferida Wolff**
illustrated by **Joung Un Kim**

January **snow** is falling.
Kiko slips in the snow.

February is **cold** and still. Kiko's window is frosted white. Kiko draws a smile with her finger. The smile melts the ice.

Kiko's hat flies off! March wind whips Kiko's hair. "I am the wind," says Kiko.

April **rain** falls everywhere. It waters the earth and Kiko, too. Now she must play inside.

Kiko plants a seed. Maybe it will grow big. May is a **month** for growing.

Kiko picks June strawberries. One fat berry for the basket. Many fat berries for Kiko. Inside they become Kikoberries.

July fireflies glow in the night. They blink their lights at Kiko. Kiko chases them and laughs. Her eyes are shining, too.

August mornings are **hot**. Kiko wears her bathing suit. She sits in her pool. Now August feels **cool**.

Crickets chirp at Kiko. Together they sing a September song.

Red and gold leaves are falling. Kiko holds a red leaf in one hand. She holds a gold leaf in the other. Kiko feels like an October tree.

Kiko looks for the moon. The orange moon is hiding. When Kiko hides, the moon finds her. Kiko and the November moon are playing.

In December Kiko breathes out clouds. She puts on her winter coat. She wears her mittens and hat. Kiko is ready for snow. ❖

Meet the Author

Ferida Wolff

Ferida Wolff wrote a lot when she was a young girl. She wrote about people and pets. She wrote letters and stories.

Ms. Wolff still writes many stories. There is always something new to learn and write about.

▲ Ferida Wolff

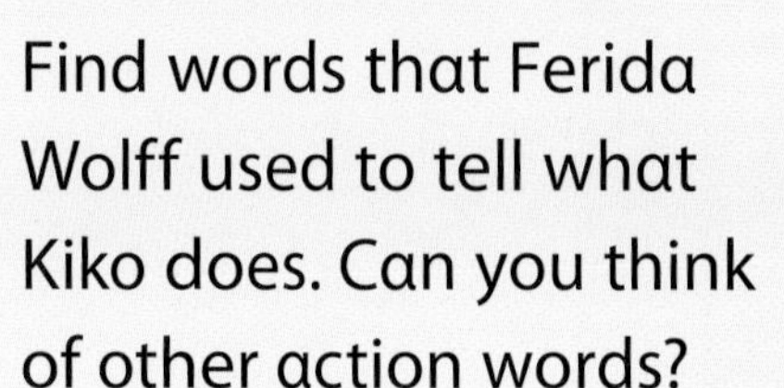

Writer's Craft

Find words that Ferida Wolff used to tell what Kiko does. Can you think of other action words?

Talk About It

1. What does Kiko do in the **month** of May?

   Kiko ______ in the month of May.

2. Why does Kiko wear a hat and gloves when she plays in the **snow**?

   She wears them because ______ .

3. Does Kiko like July? How do you know?

   Kiko ______ July. She ______ .

Learn test-taking strategies.
NGReach.com

Write About It

Find one sensory detail in *A Year for Kiko.*
Fill in these sentences.

The sensory detail word is ______ .
This tells me Kiko ______ .

Classify Details

What does Kiko do in different weather?

Classification Chart

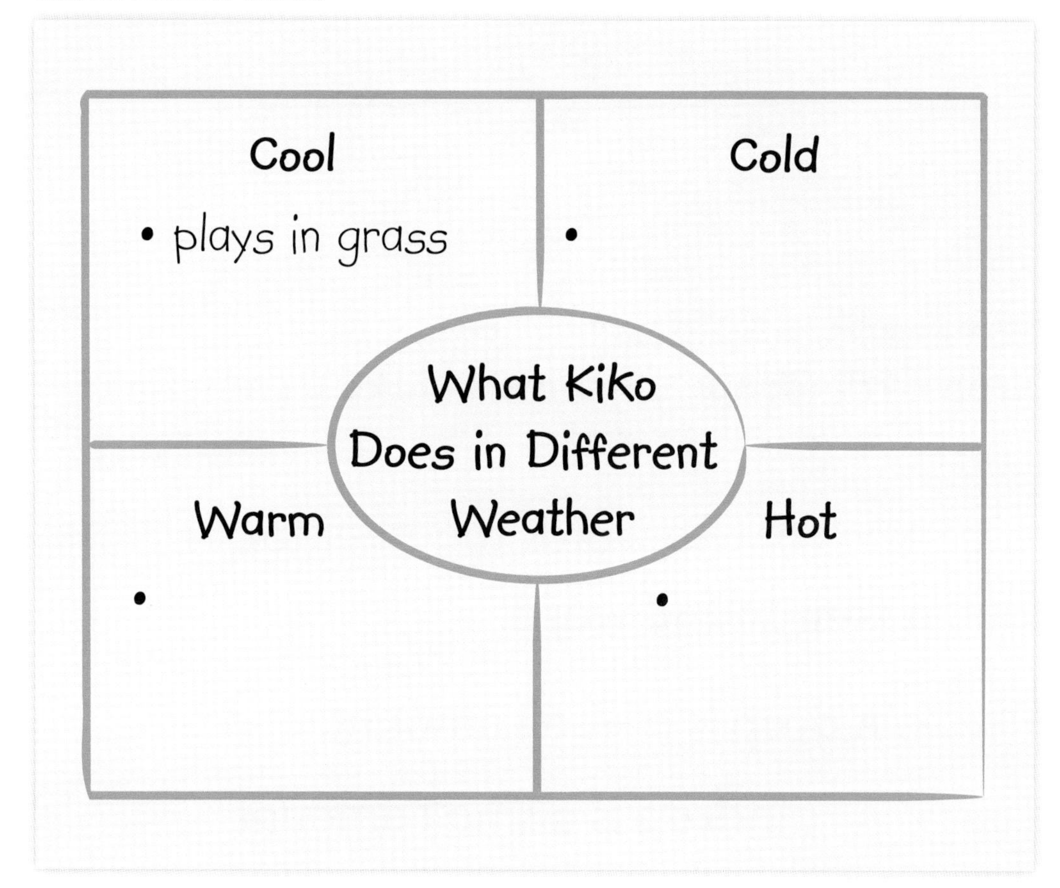

Use your chart and the illustrations in the story to retell what Kiko does in different weather.

Compound Words

raindrop
snowflake
rain + drop = raindrop
snow + flake = snowflake

Put the meanings of two words together to understand a **compound word**.

drop • A **drop** is a small amount.

rain + drop • A **raindrop** is a small amount of rain.

Try It Together

Put these words together to make compound words. Use what you know about each word to tell what it means.

fire	+	flies	=	fireflies
Kiko	+	berries	=	Kikoberries
moon	+	light	=	moonlight

Connect Across Texts Learn more about how weather can be wild.

Genre In an **interview**, one person asks questions while another person answers them.

Chasing Storms with Tim Samaras

by **Jennifer Tetzloff**

Most people run from tornadoes. Not Tim Samaras. He is a storm chaser.

What is a storm chaser?

A storm chaser follows thunderstorms that create tornadoes to learn more about them.

What is a tornado?

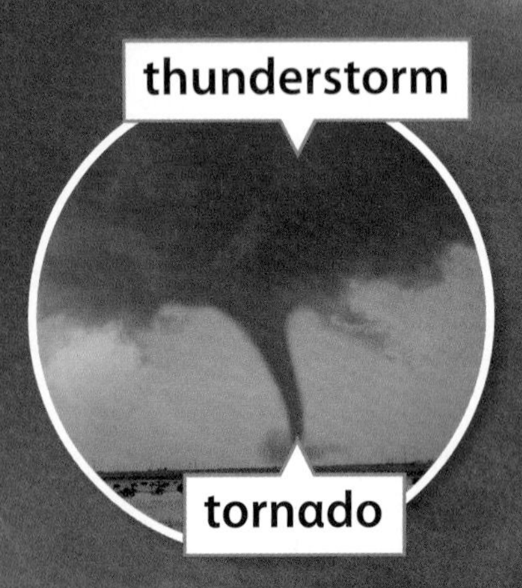

A tornado starts as a powerful thunderstorm. The storm creates spinning, funnel-shaped clouds. If the clouds touch the ground, then it is a tornado.

Where and when do tornadoes happen?

Tornadoes can happen anywhere. Most tornadoes happen between March and August.

Why do you study tornadoes?

Tornadoes are dangerous. Learning about tornadoes helps keep people safe. ❖

Compare Genres

How are the words in *A Year for Kiko* and "Chasing Storms with Tim Samaras" different?

Realistic Fiction

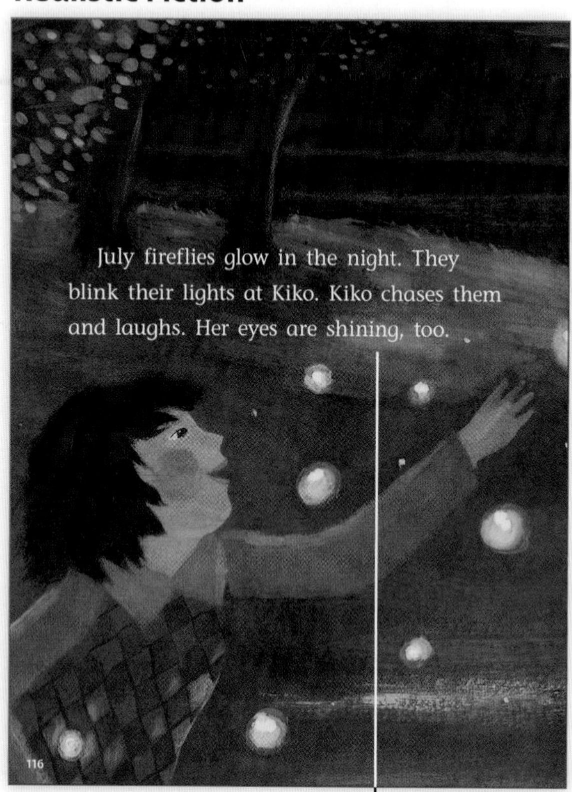

July fireflies glow in the night. They blink their lights at Kiko. Kiko chases them and laughs. Her eyes are shining, too.
116

has sensory details and characters

Interview

has facts about real people

Talk Together

Think about what you read. What's wild about weather?

Ask Questions

Ask a **question** to get **information**.

Grammar Rules **Ask Questions**

Questions	Information
Who is that?	That is Tim.
What is that?	It is a tornado.
Where is the tornado?	It is far away.
Why is it so windy?	It is windy because of the tornado.
When did it start raining?	It started at 4:00.
How is the weather?	It is rainy.

Read a Sentence

What information do these questions ask about? How do you know?

1. Who is a storm chaser?
2. When can I meet Tim?

Write a Sentence

Write a question for Tim. Ask him for information about his job.

Write Like a Reporter

Write a Nonfiction Paragraph

What do you know about weather? Explain what happens on a windy, rainy, sunny, or snowy day. Write a paragraph for your classmates.

A paragraph has an indent.

A Rainy Day

Kids wear raincoats. They jump in puddles. You hear thunder. Boom! This all happens because the weather is rainy. Rain falls from the sky.

A nonfiction paragraph tells something real that happens.

It also tells why things happen.

❶ Plan and Write

Language Frames

- ____ happens because the weather is ____.

Talk about kinds of weather with a partner. Pick one kind of weather. Explain to your partner what happens because of this weather.

Write a sentence that tells the kind of weather. Then write sentences to explain what happens because of this weather.

❷ Check Your Work

Revise and edit your writing. Use this checklist.

Checklist

- ☑ Did you use any compound words? Can you add one?
- ☑ Check your sentences. Did you use the right end marks?
- ☑ Read each word of your paragraph. Check the spelling. Look for missing letters. Correct spelling errors.

❸ Finish and Share

Finish your paragraph. Write each sentence neatly. Leave space between each word.

Read your paragraph clearly. Listen politely when other reporters read.

Sometimes we hear thunder on a rainy day.

BIG Question
What's wild about weather?

Share Your Ideas

Think about the different kinds of weather. What's wild about weather? Choose one of these ways to share your ideas about the **Big Question**.

Write It!
Draw and Write
Draw a picture of a storm. Write two sentences about the storm. Tell how it looks and sounds.
The sky is dark. The thunder is loud.

Talk About It! 

Weather Report

Pretend that you are a weather person on TV. Give your weather report to the group. Describe the weather today. Tell what the weather will be like tomorrow.

Today it is sunny and warm.

Do It!

Make Air Move

With a partner make a fan, kite, or other type of air mover. Explain to your partner how your invention works.

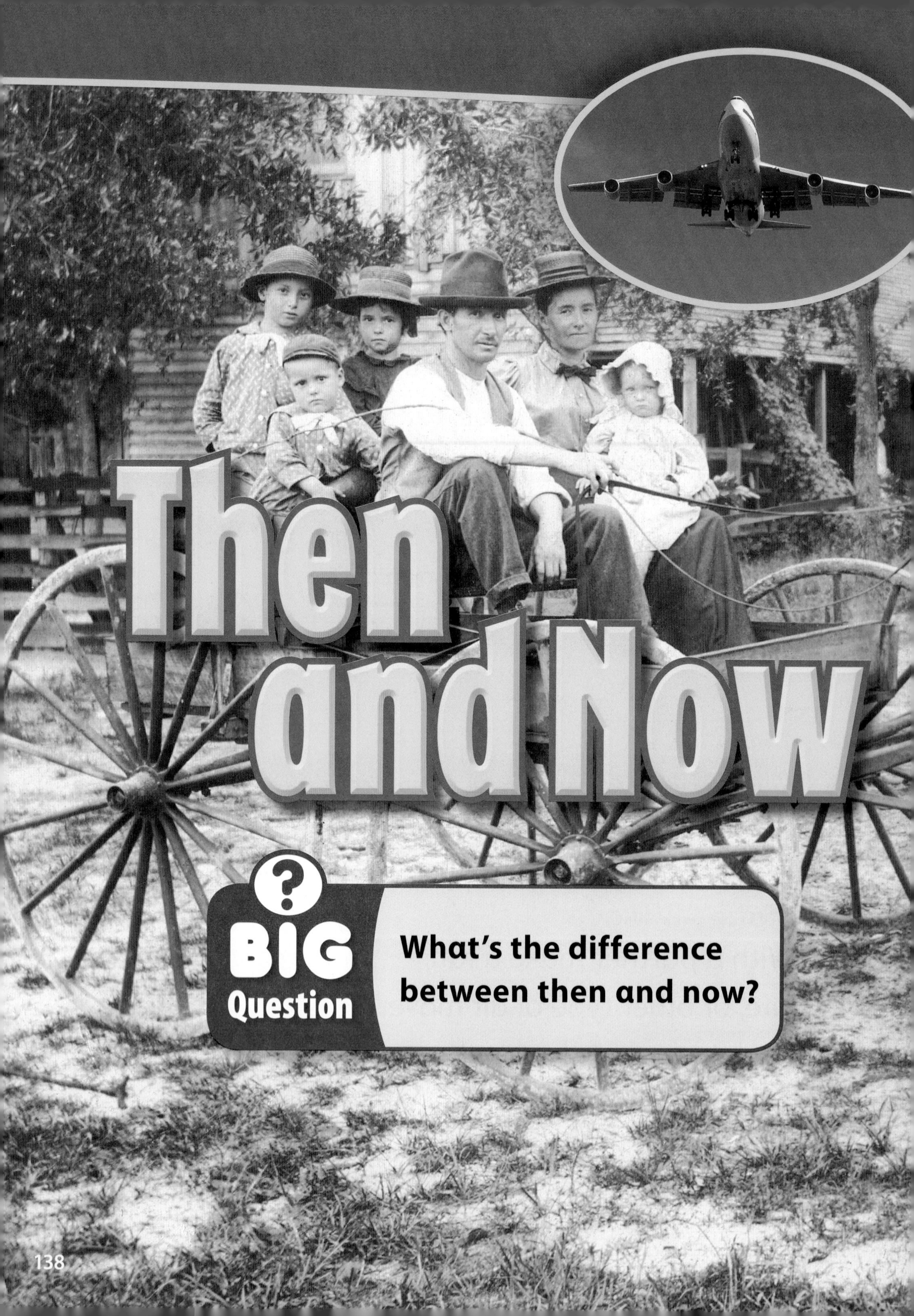
Then and Now
BIG Question
What's the difference between then and now?

Unit at a Glance

- **Language**: Express Opinions, Express Feelings, Social Studies Words
- **Literacy**: Visualize
- **Content**: Then and Now

Unit 7

Share What You Know

Do It!

1. **Act Out** something you do with a machine. Let the class guess.
2. **Discuss** what people did before they had that machine.

Build Background: Watch a video about an invention.

NGReach.com

High Frequency Words
do
not
think

Express Opinions

Listen and sing. **Song** MP3

Call Me

I think it would be great
To hear your voice.
I think it would be great
To hear your voice.

You could write a letter.
But I think
The phone is better.

I do not think a letter
Is a good choice.

Tune: "If You're Happy and You Know It"

Key Words

How do people talk and share **news**?

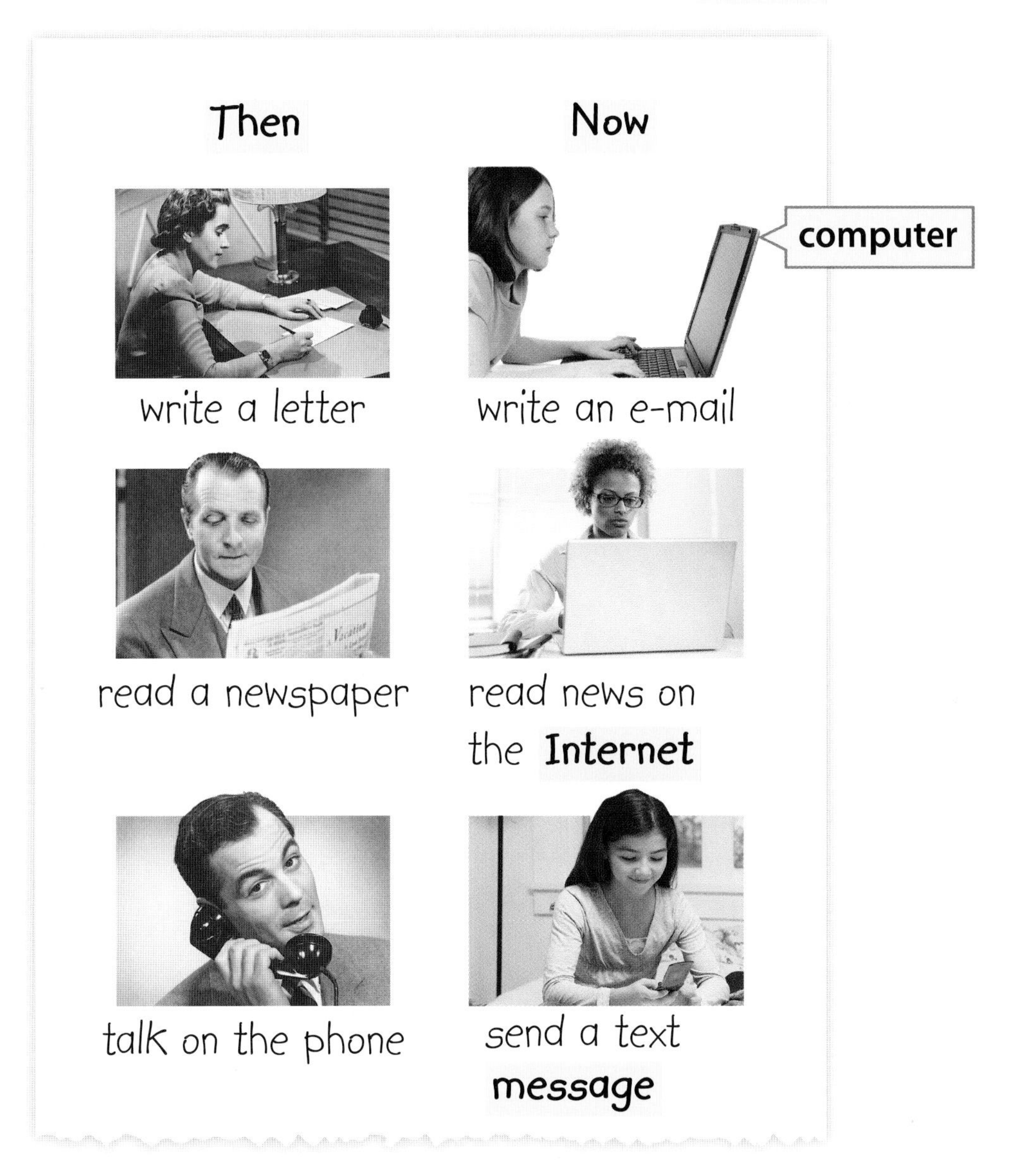

Talk Together

Look at the ways we communicate. What's the difference between then and now? What do you think is the best way to communicate?

Identify Main Idea and Details

Main Idea and Details Diagram

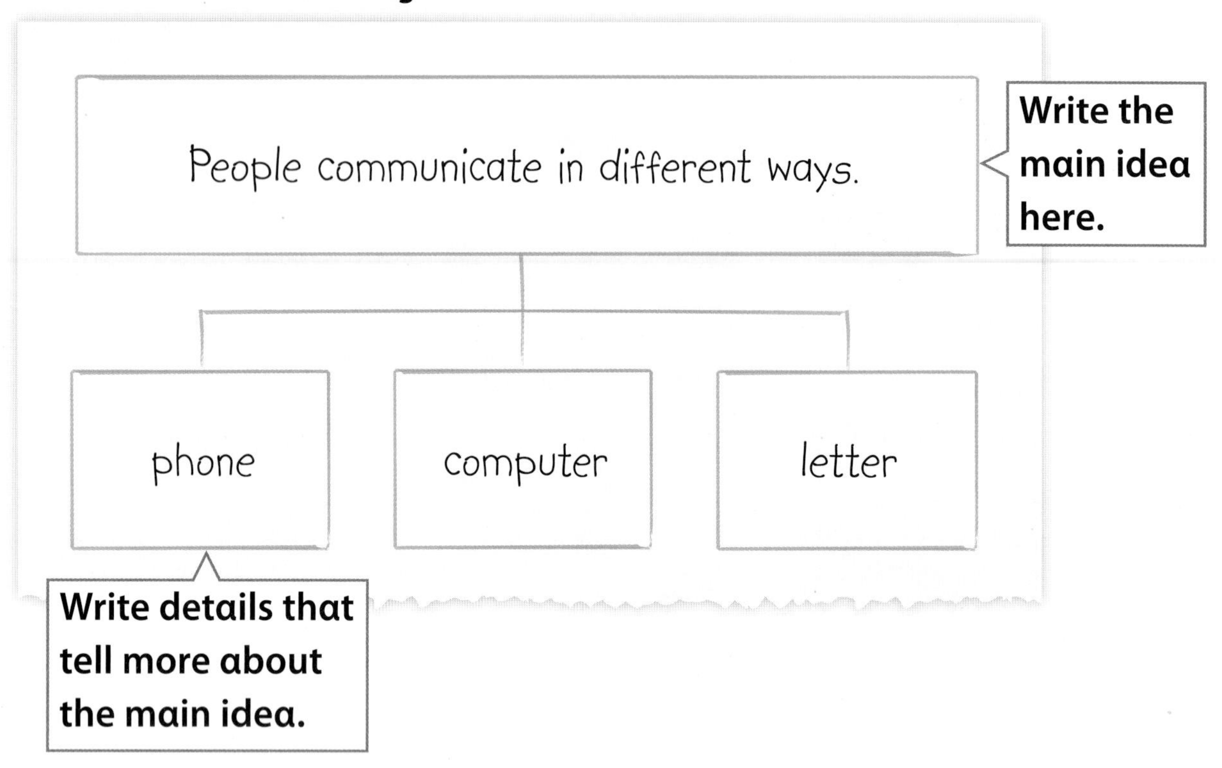
People communicate in different ways.
Write the main idea here.
phone
computer
letter
Write details that tell more about the main idea.

Look for the main idea and details as you listen and read.

Talk Together

Use gestures to show how you communicate. Your partner guesses what you are doing. Take turns. Then add ways you communicate to the chart.

More Key Words

past | **present** | **future**

In the **past** I was in kindergarten.

Today is the **present**. I am in first grade.

In the **future** I will be in second grade.

communicate

People **communicate** by talking and writing.

history

Study **history** to learn what happened long ago.

Talk Together

Make **Key Word** cards. Pick one, and use the word in a sentence.

I learn about the present by watching today's TV news.

Add words to My Vocabulary Notebook.
NGReach.com

Read a History Article

A **history article** is nonfiction. It describes what life was like in the past.

Time Line

A time line shows when things happened.

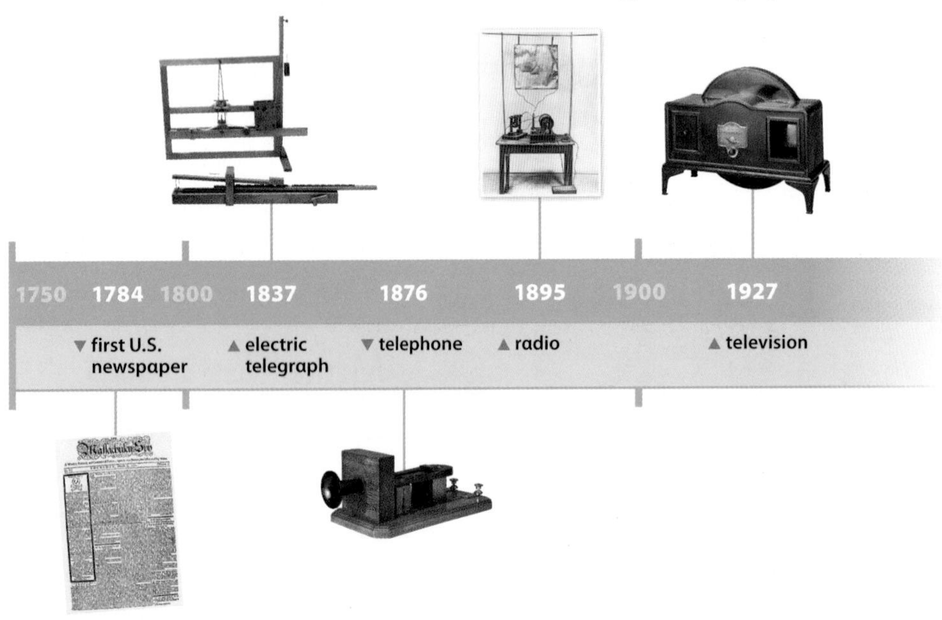

▲ This time line shows years.

Reading Strategy

As you read, use the words and pictures to **visualize** what things were like in the past.

Communication
Then and Now

by **Robin Nelson**

Comprehension Coach

Communication is sharing ideas and **news**.

Most people **communicate** by talking and writing.

People can use their bodies to communicate, too.

Communication has changed. People **now** communicate better and faster.

Long ago, people made pictures to tell stories. The pictures could be drawings or symbols.

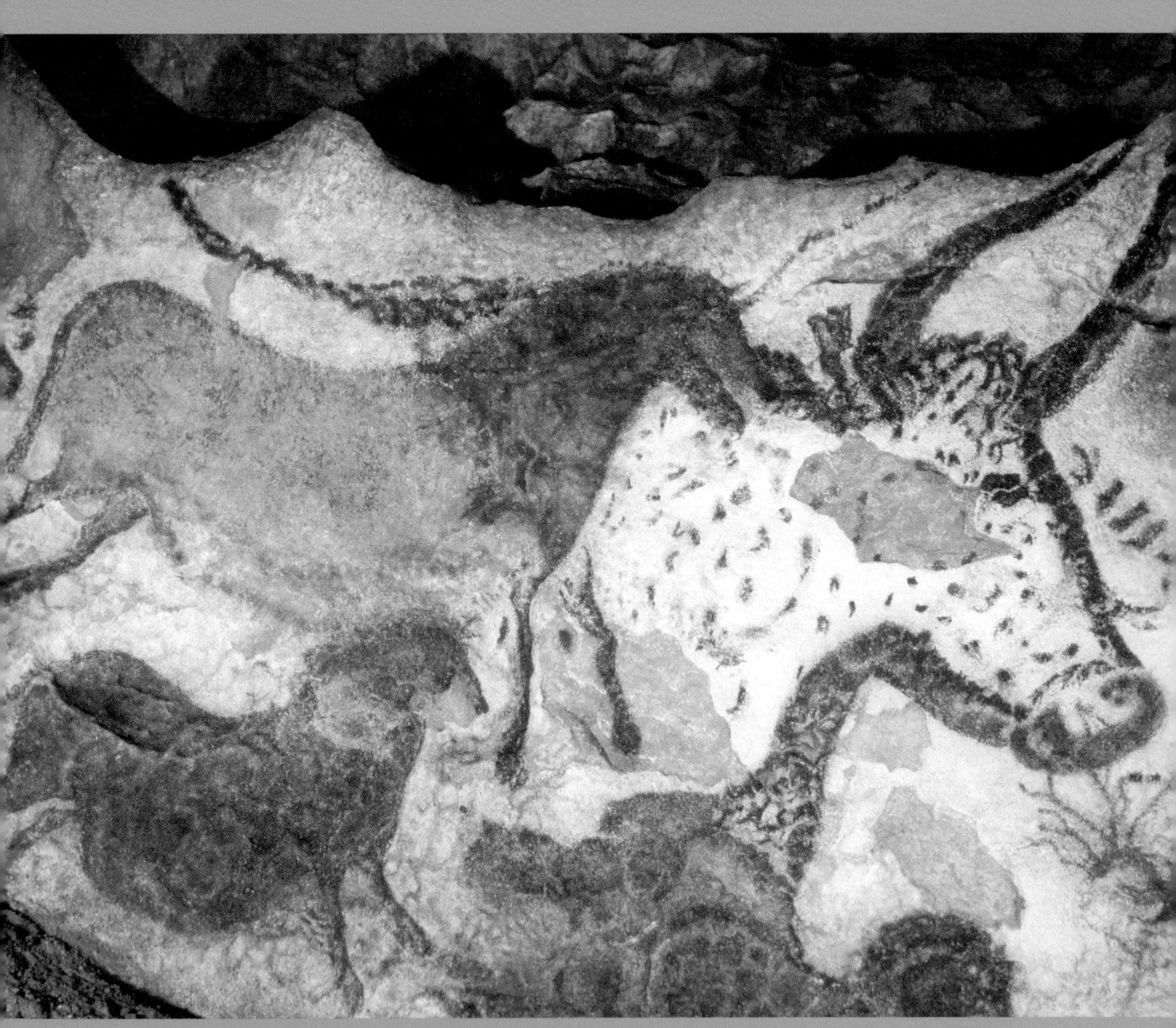

▲ This painting was discovered in a cave in France.

There are over 170,000 words in the English language.

Now, people use words more often to tell stories.

Long ago, people copied each book. If they wanted 10 copies of a book, they had to write out each copy one at a time.

▲ **This book was written with a feather pen and bottles of ink in 1453.**

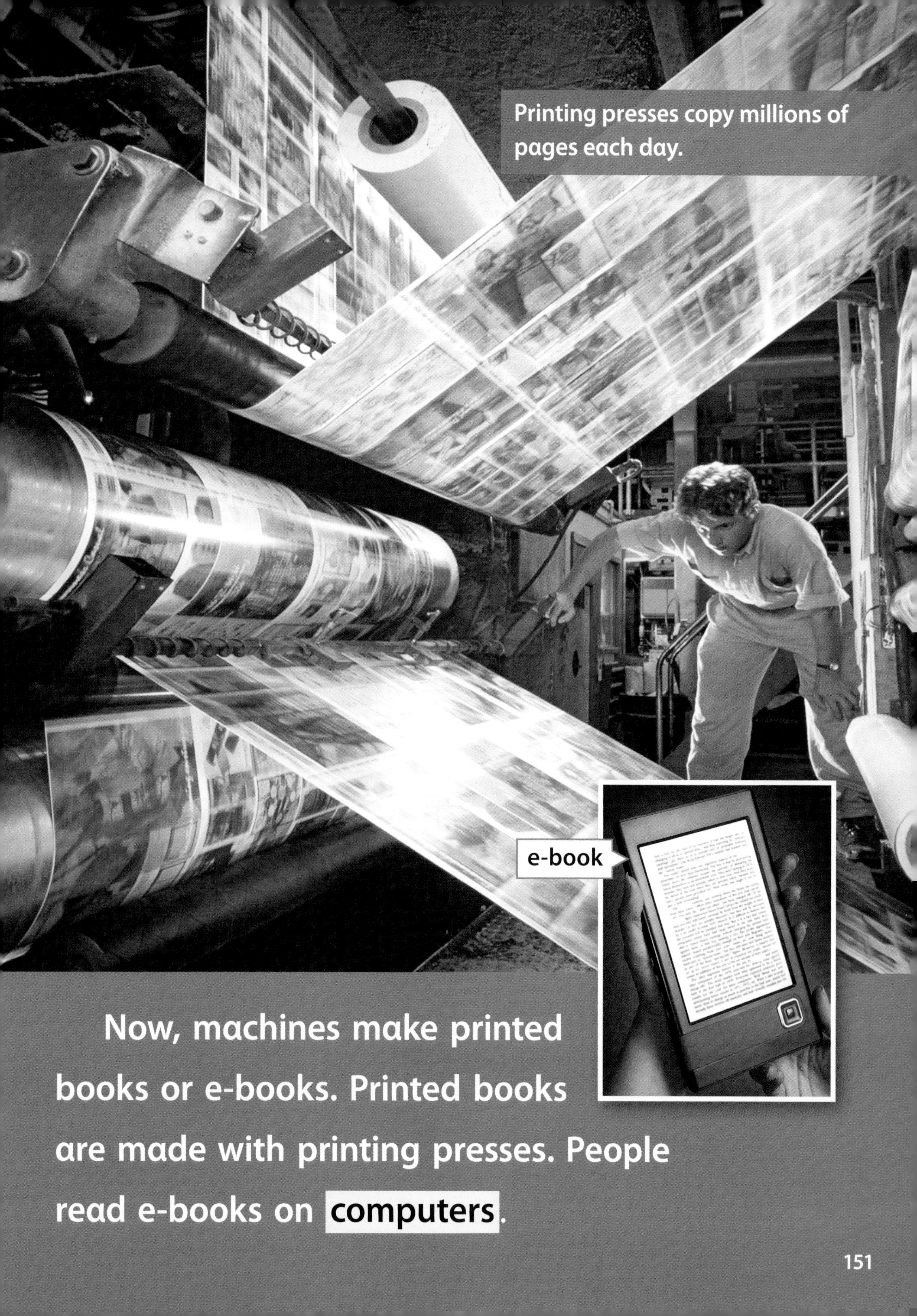

Printing presses copy millions of pages each day.

Now, machines make printed books or e-books. Printed books are made with printing presses. People read e-books on **computers**.

Long ago, people tapped **messages** on telegraph machines. Telegraph machines sent messages using electricity. It took about a minute to send each word.

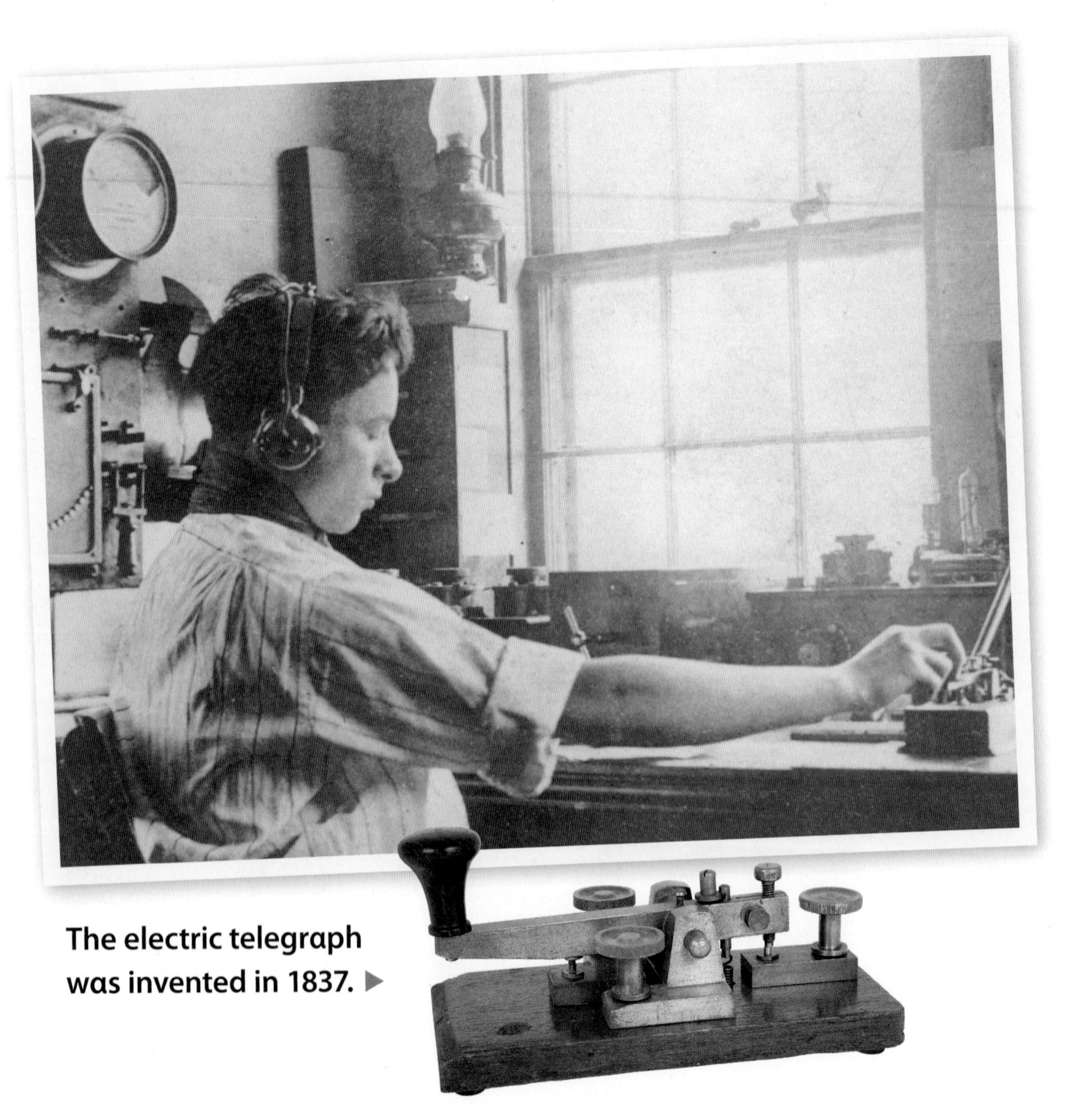

The electric telegraph was invented in 1837. ▶

▼ The telephone was invented in 1876 by Alexander Graham Bell.

Now, people call each other on telephones. Most people have mobile phones. Long ago, telephones always needed cords.

Long ago, people wrote letters. It could take months to mail a letter. Mail went on ships and by horses. Today, mail delivery is done by trucks and planes so letters are delivered much quicker.

▲ People wrote letters using pens and paper.

e-mail message

Now, people write e-mails on computers. An e-mail message can be delivered in just seconds. Today, many people write e-mail messages instead of hand-written letters.

The Monthly Reporter

VOL. 1. MONTPELIER, VT., FEBRUARY, NO. 2.

Newspapers were sold on street corners. This newspaper was sold in New York in 1896.

Long ago, hundreds of people read newspapers. The first United States daily newspaper was published in 1784. People had to buy a newspaper to read it.

Now, millions of people read newspapers. People can buy printed newspapers.

People can also read newspapers on the **Internet**. People all over the world can read news on the Internet.

Long ago, people could only listen to news on radios. Radios only make sounds. They do not have pictures.

▲ The radio was invented in 1895.

Now, people can watch news on televisions.

Communication will continue to change. What do you think will happen next? ❖

The TV was invented in 1927.

Communication Timeline

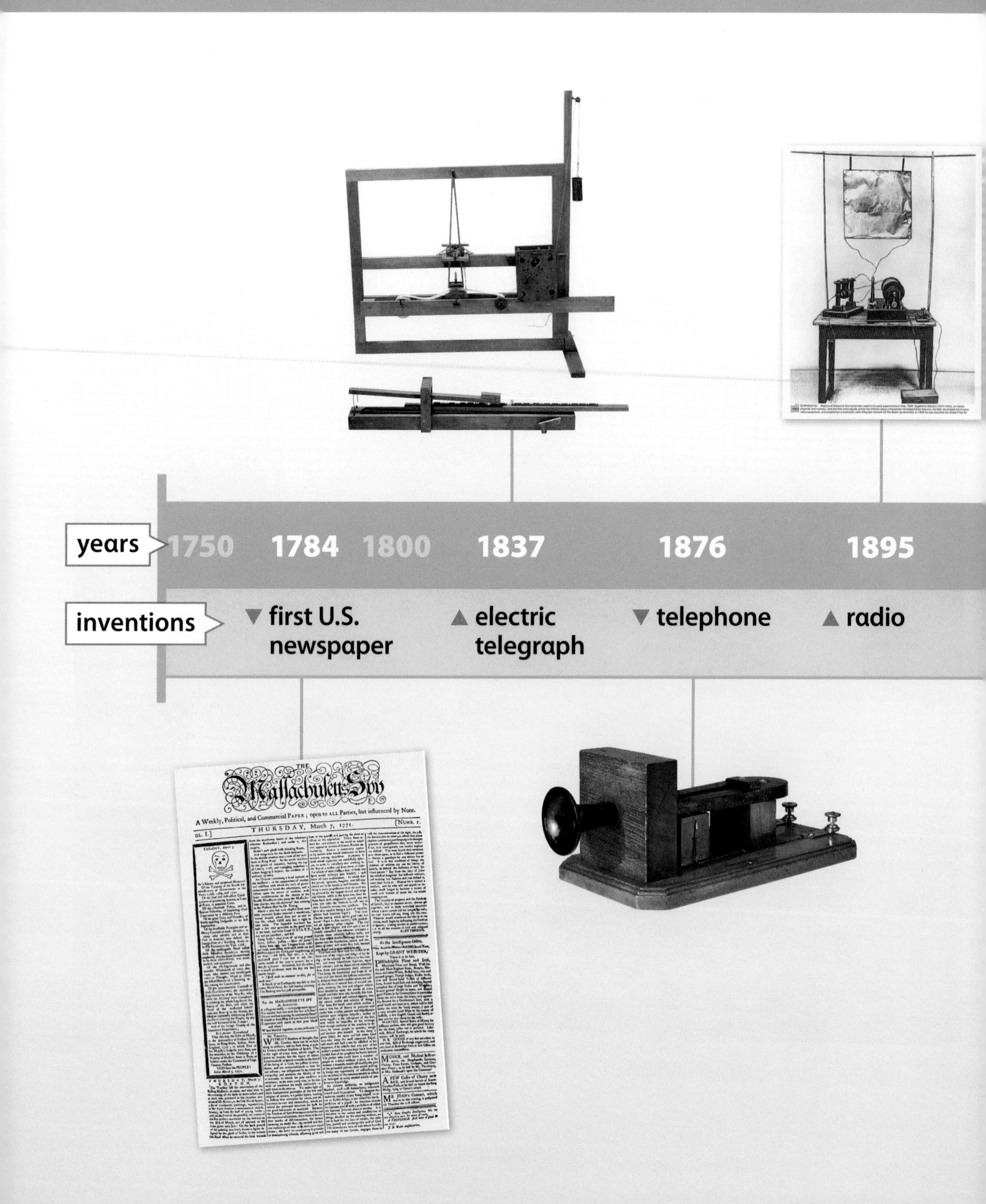

1900	1927	1943	1972	1985	2000
	▲ television	▼ computer	▲ e-mail	▼ first cell phones used	

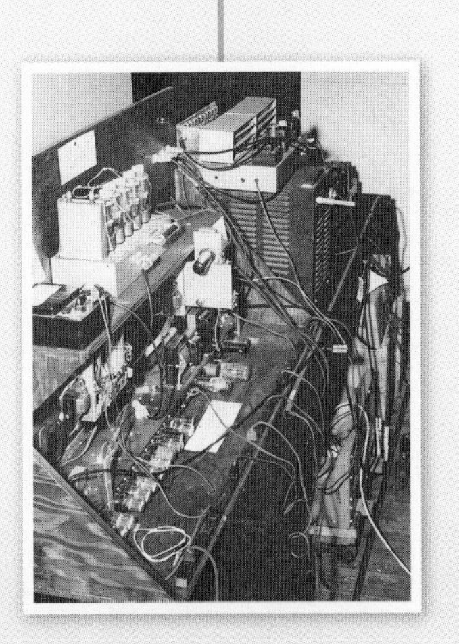

Talk About It 

1. How do people **communicate**?

   People communicate by ____ and ____ .

2. How is communication different **now** than it was in the **past**? Look back in the text, and name two details.

   Now, people ____ . Then, people ____ .

3. Why is the **computer** an important invention?

   People can ____ and ____ on a computer.

Learn test-taking strategies.
NGReach.com

Write About It 

What is your favorite way to communicate? Why?

I like to ____ because ____ .

Identify Main Idea and Details

Add details to show how communication has changed.

Main Idea and Details Diagram

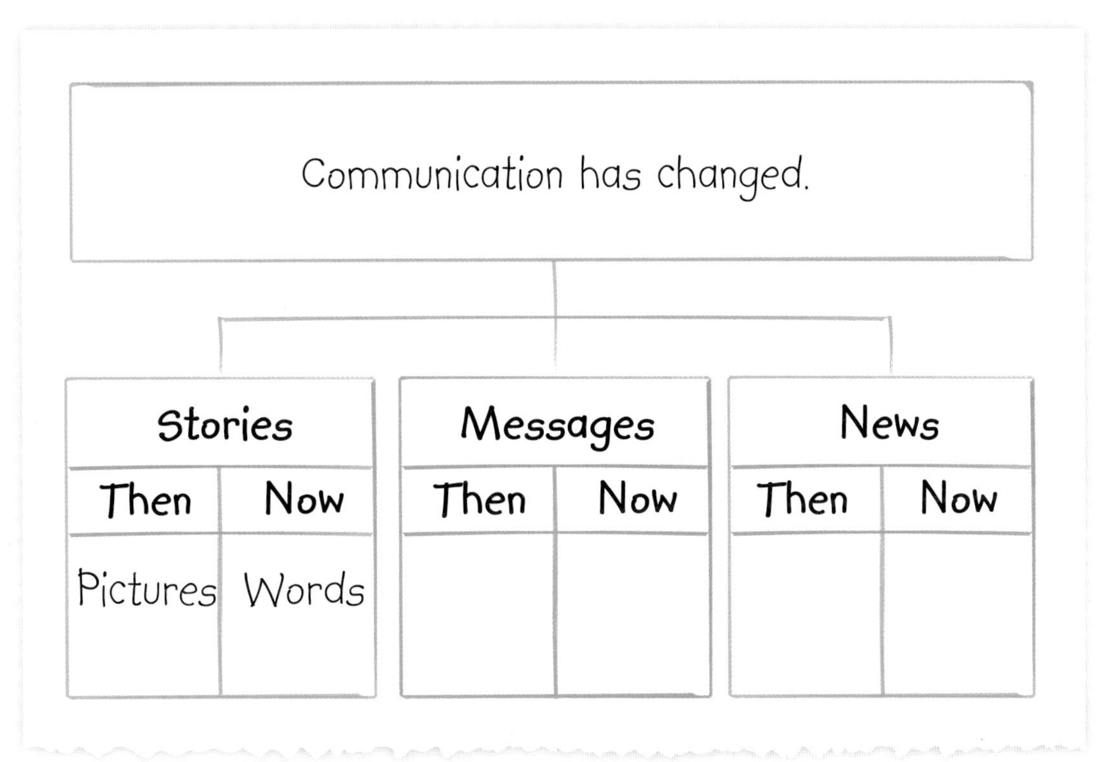

Use your chart to tell how communication has changed.

"Long ago, people drew stories with pictures."
"Now, people write stories with words."

Alphabetize and Use a Dictionary

Words in Alphabetical Order
computer
e-mail
radio
telegraph

Words in **alphabetical order** are listed by their first letters. They go in the order of the alphabet.

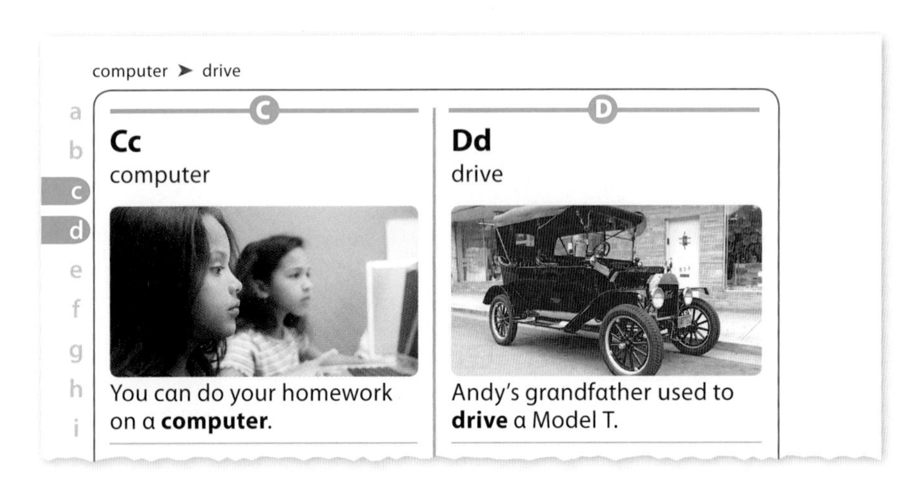

Try It Together

With a partner, put these words in alphabetical order. Use a dictionary to find each word's meaning.

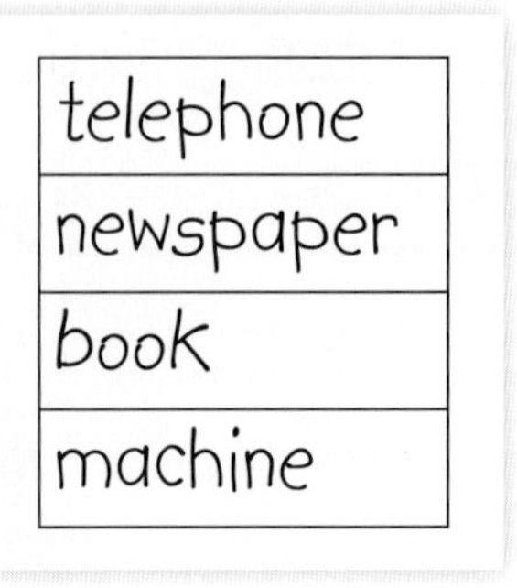

NATIONAL GEOGRAPHIC EXCLUSIVE

Connect Across Texts You read about **communication now** and in the **past**. Now read about inventions for the **future**.

Genre A **blog** is an **Internet** journal. This **blog entry** is nonfiction. It gives information about space inventions.

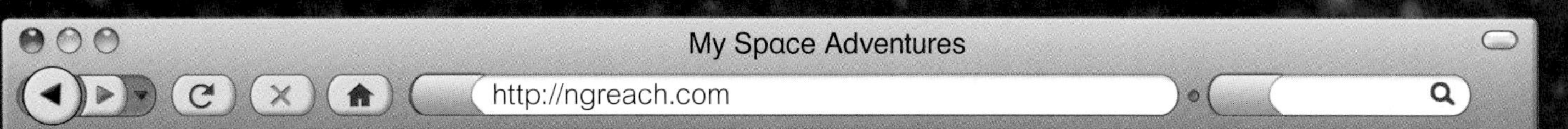

My Space Adventures

MAIN SCREEN | PICTURES | LINKS | SIGN IN

Date: August 21

Building for Space

My name is Constance Adams. I make things to use in space.

▲ Astronauts train for space travel in this model.

Search

LINKS

- Space News
- Astronaut News

My Space Adventures

http://ngreach.com

Space is not like earth. The air is different. People have to wear special clothing. They bring air to breathe. People float around in space. It is fun to watch!

Read More About Astronauts

Search

LINKS

- Space News
- Astronaut News

I make new inventions to use in space. I am helping to build a spaceship that astronauts will fly to the moon.

Next »

MAIN SCREEN | PICTURES | LINKS | SIGN IN

My Space Adventures

http://ngreach.com

MAIN SCREEN | PICTURES | LINKS | SIGN IN

The first spaceship that flew to the moon did not have much power. One **computer** in your classroom has more power than that spaceship did! Now, we can make more powerful spaceships.

Then: The Apollo 11 spaceship in 1969.

Search

LINKS

- Space News
- Astronaut News

It is fun to imagine what we will be able to make in the future!

Now: This is a computer drawing of a future spaceship being worked on. It is called Ares.

Posted by Constance Adams August 24 9:00 a.m.

Older Posts »

MAIN SCREEN | PICTURES | LINKS | SIGN IN

Compare Genres

Think about *Communication Then and Now* and "My Space Adventures." How are they alike and different?

Venn Diagram

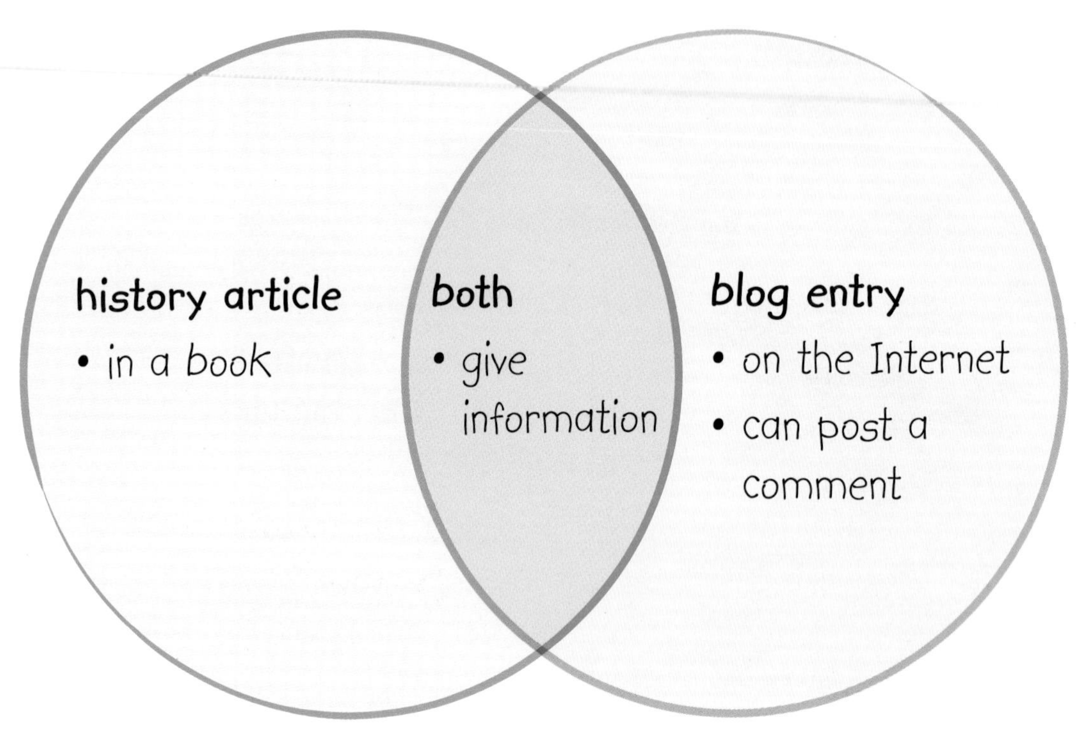

Look through the texts. Add to the diagram.

Talk Together

Think about what you read and learned. What's the difference between **then** and **now**?

Past Tense Verbs

Verbs can tell about actions that happened in the past.

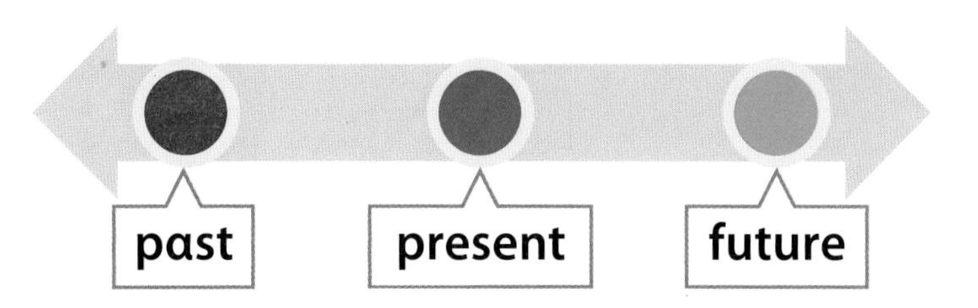

Grammar Rules Past Tense Verbs

To make a verb about the past:	
• Add -**ed** to the end of a **regular verb**, like **want**.	Today people **want** to build new spaceships. In the past, they **wanted** to build the first spaceship.
• Use a special form for an **irregular verb**, like **fly**.	Today people **fly** to space. In the past, they **flew** to space for the first time.

Read a Sentence

Read page 150. Find two verbs in the past tense. Explain their form.

Write a Sentence 

Write a sentence about a time you wanted to go somewhere new. Read it to a partner.

High Frequency
Words

am
could
feel

Express Feelings

Listen and Sing. *Song* MP3

New Phone

Oh, my darling. I am Marta.
My new phone is very small.
I wish I could have my old phone.
It was always on the wall.

My new phone is very modern.
I feel really glad for this.
I wish I could use my new phone,
But I don't know where it is.

Tune: "My Darling Clementine"

Key Words

Old

The old **record** player is fun to use.

New

But the new way to play **music** sounds **better**. It is **easier** to carry with you.

Talk Together

How would you feel about listening to music on a record player? Are new ways always better?

Describe Characters' Feelings

Character Description Chart

Character	What the Character Says or Does	What this Shows About How the Character Feels
Marta	• I wish I could have my old phone. • I feel very glad for this.	• unhappy • happy

Write the name of the character here.

Write what the character says or does here.

Write how the character feels here.

I feel sad that I don't have those shoes anymore.

Talk Together

What do you wish you could have from the past? Describe your feelings about it to a partner.

More Key Words

build

You can **build** things with blocks.

invent

People **invent** things like the telephone.

machine

This **machine** washes dishes.

modern

This cell phone is more **modern** than the old phone.

tool

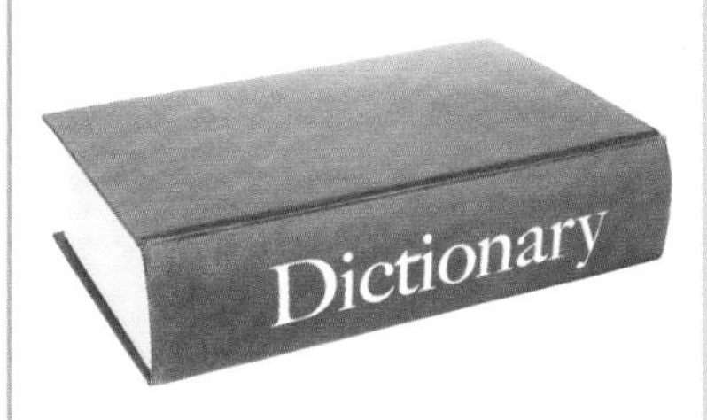

People use a dictionary as a **tool** to understand words.

Talk Together

Draw a picture of a **Key Word** for a partner to label.

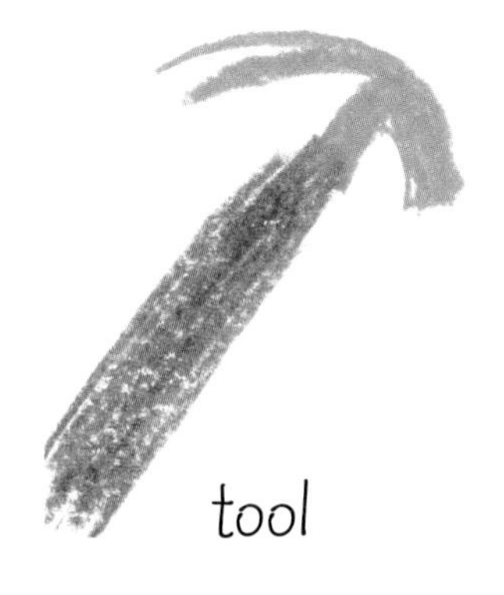

Add words to My Vocabulary Notebook.
NGReach.com

Read a Story

Realistic fiction has events that are not real but could happen in real life.

Characters' Feelings

Look for words that tell you how characters feel. Then think about why the characters have these feelings.

"I love music just like you do."

Reading Strategy

As you read, use the words and pictures to **visualize** how the characters feel and why.

A New Old Tune

by **Pat Cummings**

illustrated by
Frank Morrison

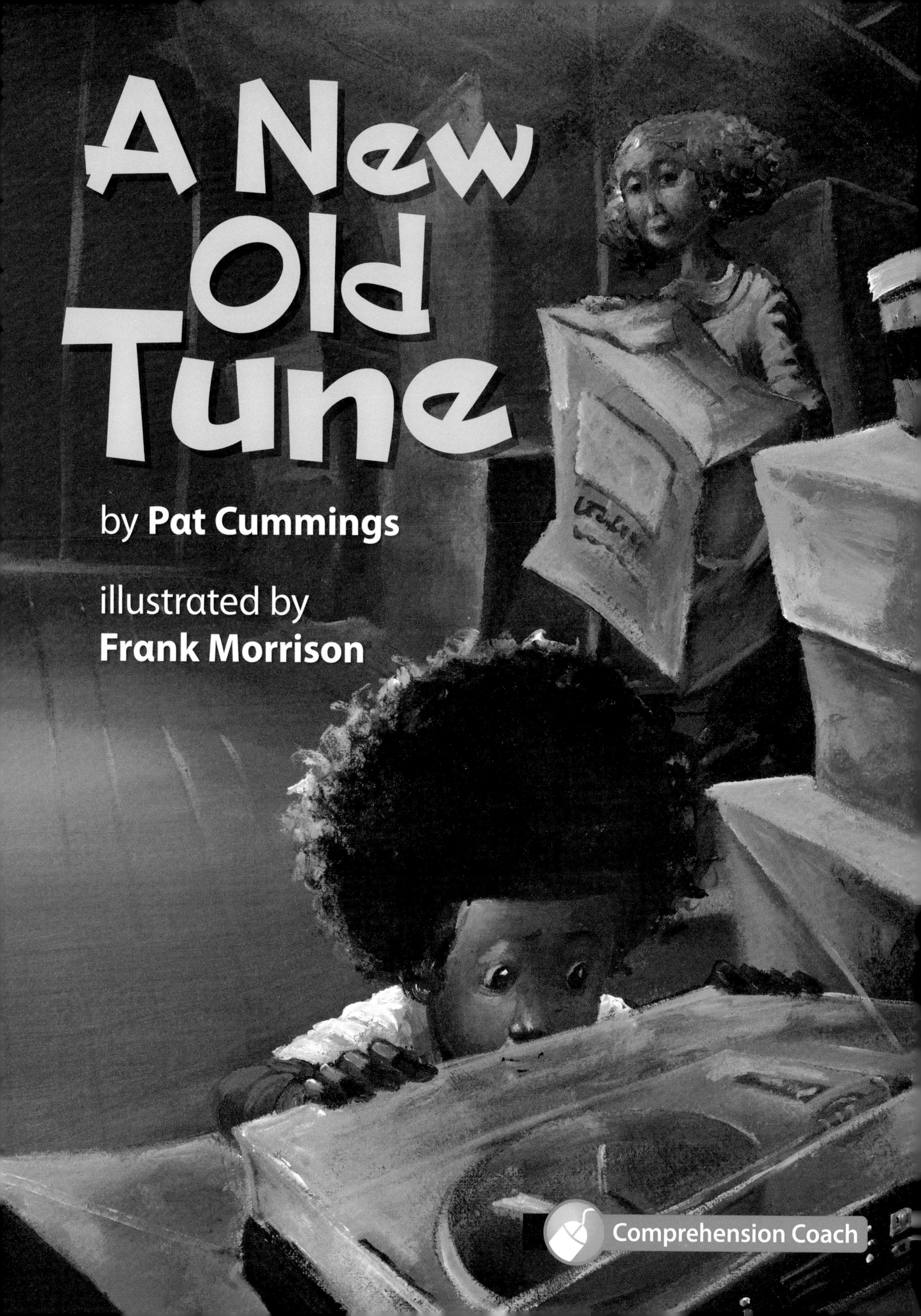

Comprehension Coach

"What is this, Aunt Nell?" asked Max. He was helping his aunt choose things to sell at her yard sale.

"This disk must go into a giant computer!" Max said. Aunt Nell shook her head.

"That is a **record**," Aunt Nell said. "I love **music** just like you do."

Aunt Nell pulled out a stack of black disks.

"Wow," said Max. "How do they work?"

Aunt Nell opened a dusty, wooden box. She plugged it into the wall. "This is my old record player."

Music filled the attic.

"But you can't carry it with you!" Max said.

"No one carried music players back then," Aunt Nell said. "I played music on this record player at home. My friends would listen, too. Then we would dance together."

“Things change,” Aunt Nell said. “Television used to be just black and white.”

“You had TV way back then?” Max asked.

“Hey, I’m not that old!” Aunt Nell said.

Max and Aunt Nell got back to work. There was an old camera she wanted to sell. There were photo albums she wanted to keep.

Max saw a picture of a young Aunt Nell talking on a phone. It had a long, curly cord.

"Did you like those old phones **better**?" Max asked.

"No," Aunt Nell smiled. "Some **new** things are much **easier** to use."

"But some old things are pretty neat," Max said. He looked at the record player. "Will you dance with me?" Max asked.

"Yes," said Aunt Nell. She turned up the music.

"Has anything stayed the same?" asked Max.

"Yes," said Aunt Nell. "People still love to talk on the telephone. And watch television. And listen to music."

"And dance!" added Max.

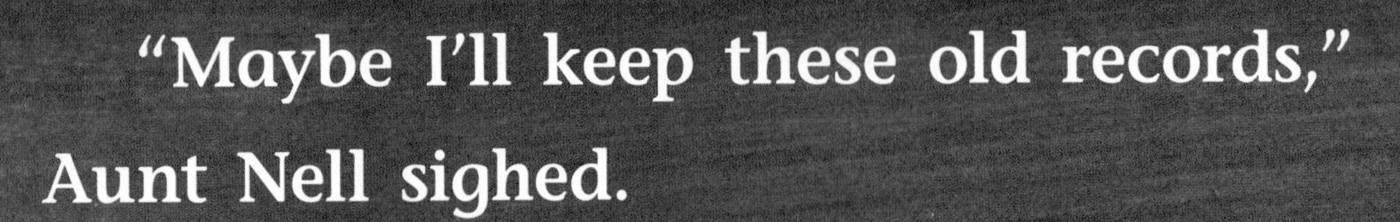

“Maybe I’ll keep these old records,” Aunt Nell sighed.

“Or you could burn them onto a music player,” Max said.

“BURN them?” Aunt Nell gasped.

Max groaned. It was his turn to explain.

Meet the Author

AWARD WINNER

Pat Cummings

Pat Cummings moved often when she was young. Her father was in the army. She used to draw pictures all the time. She joined art clubs to meet new friends.

Ms. Cummings writes about things she knows. She is always thinking about her next story!

Pat Cummings ▶

Writer's Craft

Pat Cummings helps readers learn about her characters' feelings by using verbs. Can you find examples of this in the story?

Talk About It

1. What was Max helping Aunt Nell do?

   Max was helping Aunt Nell ____ .

2. What can Max and Aunt Nell learn from each other?

   Max can learn ____ from Aunt Nell.
   Aunt Nell can learn ____ from Max.

3. Think about your own photos. Why does Aunt Nell want to keep her photo albums?

   Aunt Nell wants to keep them because ____ .

Learn test-taking strategies.
NGReach.com

Write About It

What does your family own that is **old**? What do you think about it?

We have an old ____ . I think it is ____ .

Describe Characters' Feelings

What do Max and Nell say or do? What does this show about how they feel?

Character Description Chart

Character	What the Character Says or Does	What This Shows About How the Character Feels
Max	• Wow •	• He feels surprised. •
Nell	• •	• •

Use your chart to talk about Max and Nell. Why do they feel like they do?

Alphabetize and Use a Dictionary

Words in Alphabetical Order

camera
cell phone
cord

These words are in **alphabetical order**. Each word begins with the same letter. The second letter of each word is used to put them in order.

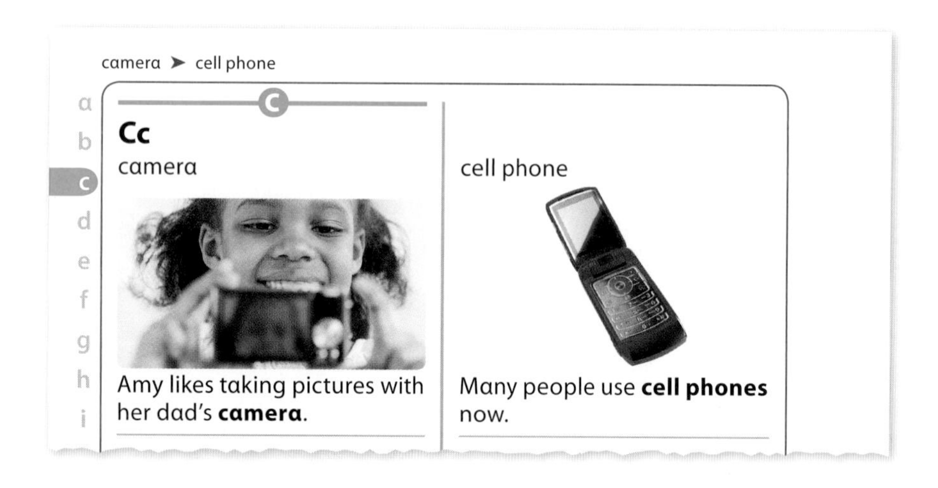

camera ➤ cell phone
a
b
c
d
e
f
g
h
i
Cc
camera
Amy likes taking pictures with her dad's **camera**.
cell phone
Many people use **cell phones** now.

Try It Together

With a partner, write these words on cards. Put the words in alphabetical order. Use a dictionary to find the word's meaning. Then read your list aloud.

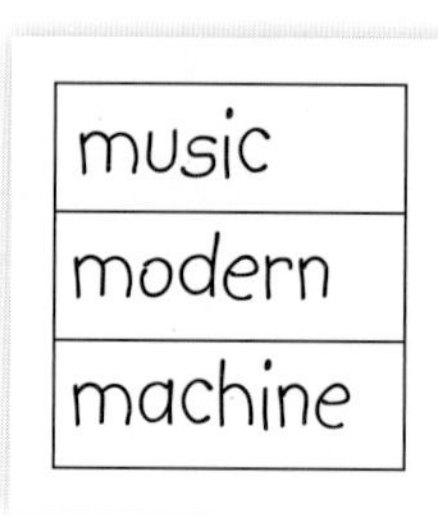

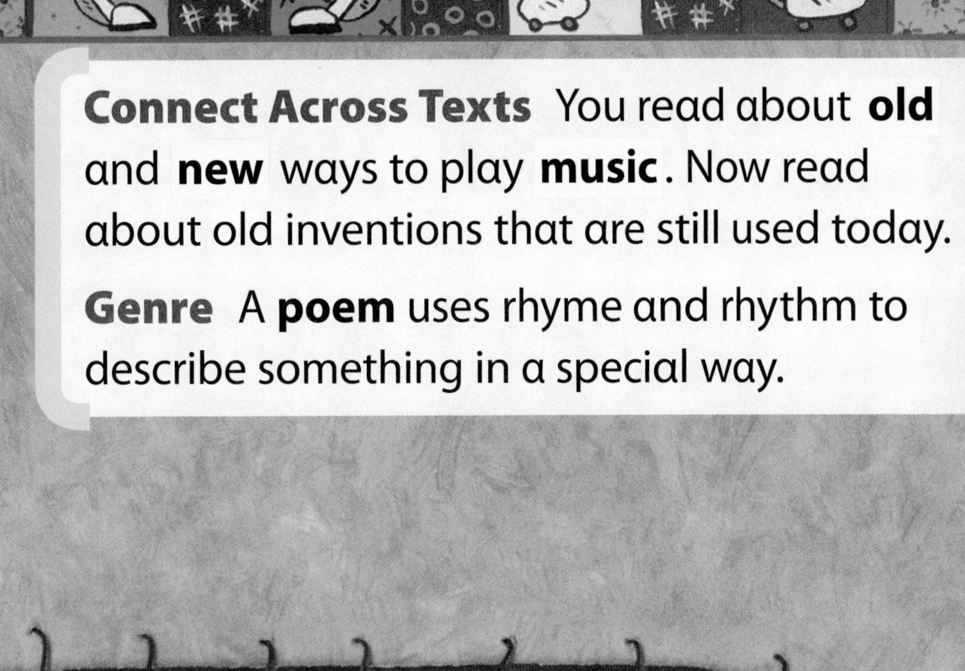

Connect Across Texts You read about **old** and **new** ways to play **music**. Now read about old inventions that are still used today.

Genre A **poem** uses rhyme and rhythm to describe something in a special way.

Invention Poems

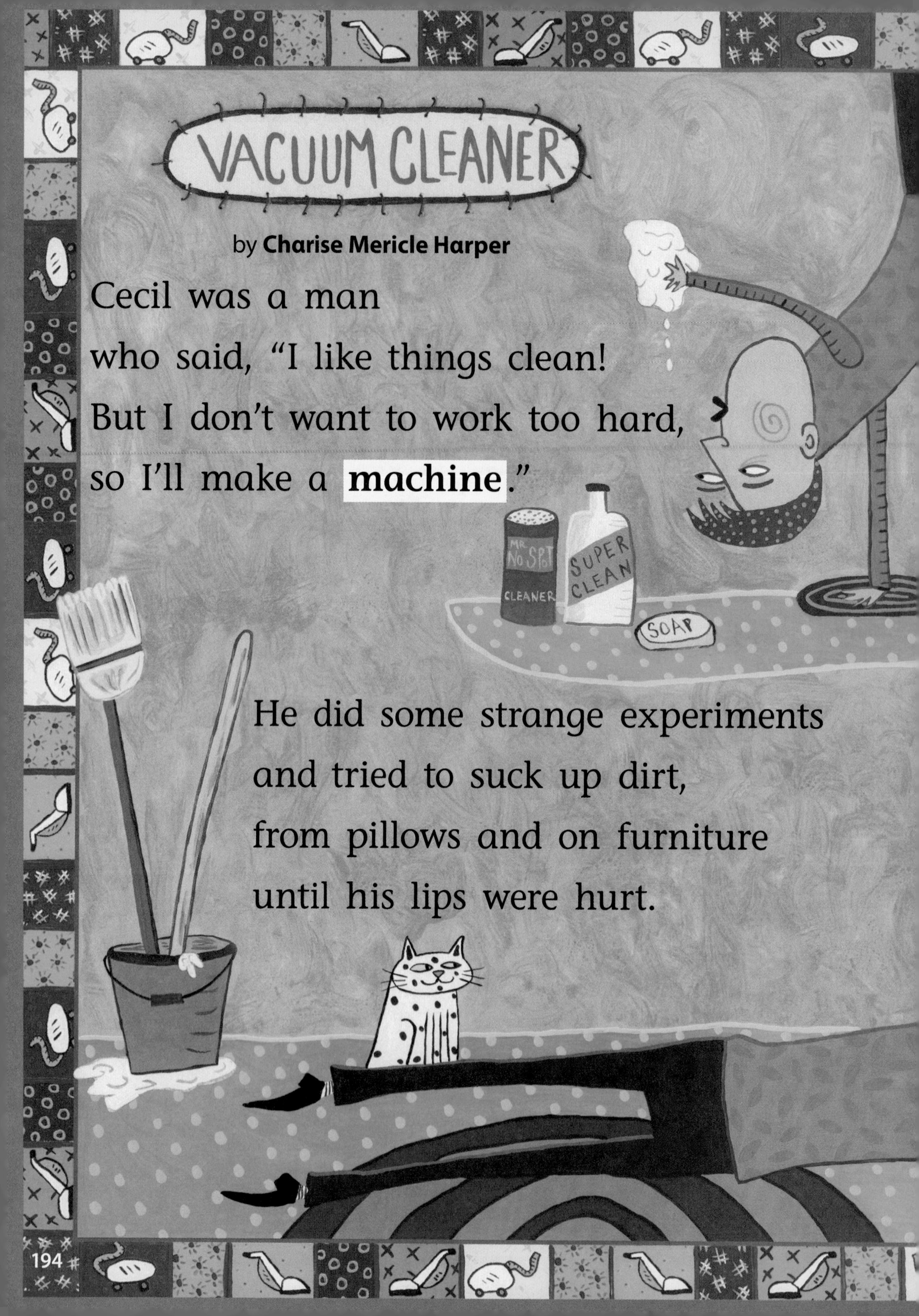

VACUUM CLEANER

by **Charise Mericle Harper**

Cecil was a man
who said, "I like things clean!
But I don't want to work too hard,
so I'll make a **machine**."

He did some strange experiments
and tried to suck up dirt,
from pillows and on furniture
until his lips were hurt.

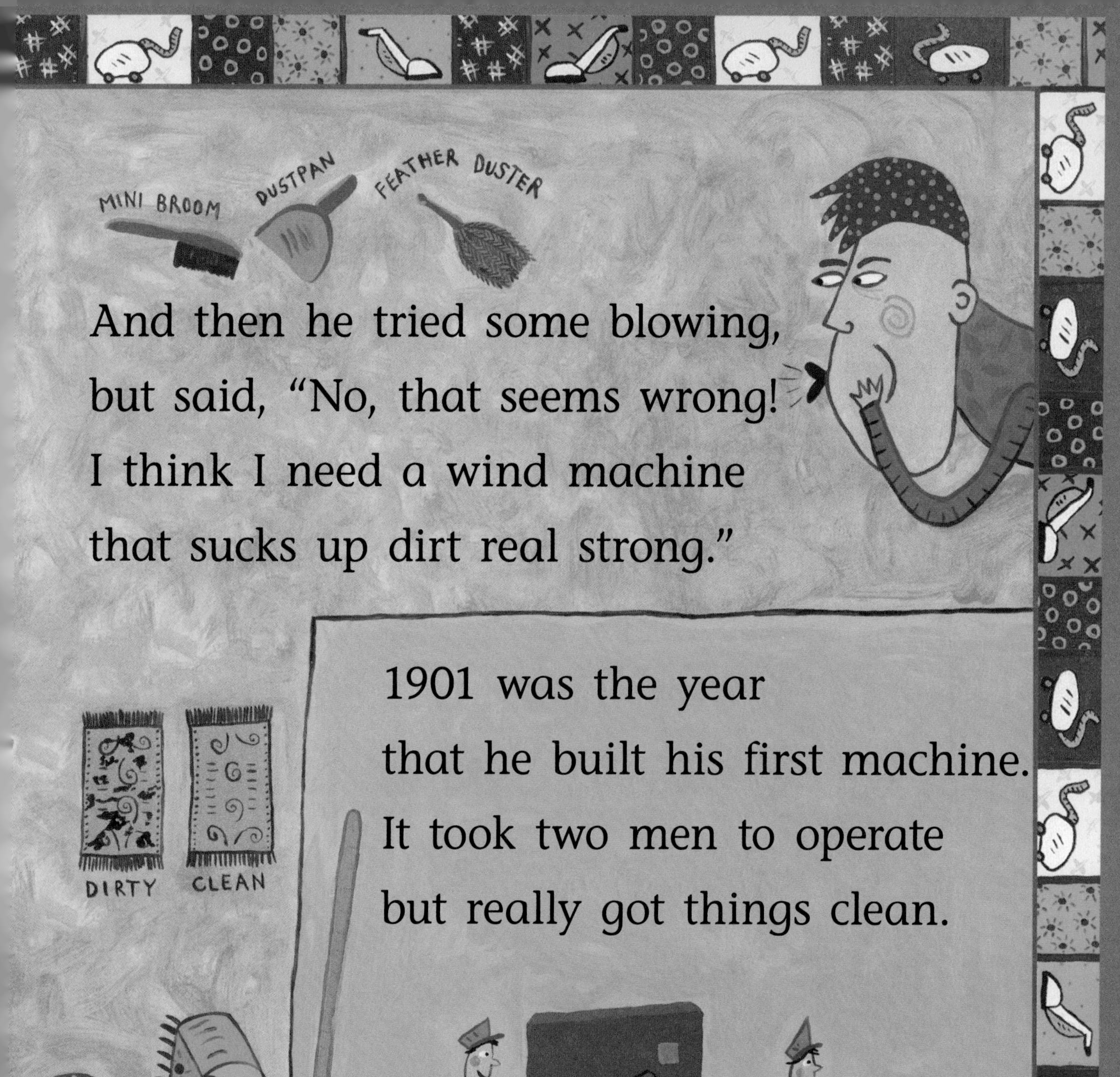

And then he tried some blowing,
but said, "No, that seems wrong!
I think I need a wind machine
that sucks up dirt real strong."

1901 was the year
that he built his first machine.
It took two men to operate
but really got things clean.

Past and Present

by **Hector Sanchez**

When I think about
The present and the past,
I think about machines
That move slow and fast.

Clunky cars used to creep
So super slow,
Now they zip and zoom
And go, go, go!

Compare Genres

A New Old Tune is realistic fiction. "Vacuum Cleaner" and "Past and Present" are poems. Find connections between these texts.

Realistic Fiction

"No one carried music players back then," Aunt Nell said. "I played music on this record player at home. My friends would listen, too. Then we would dance together."

182

Poem

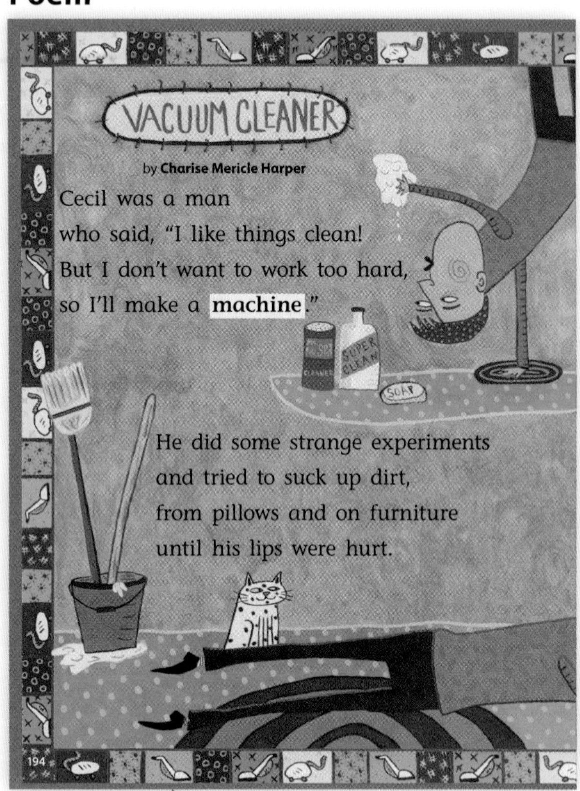
VACUUM CLEANER

by Charise Mericle Harper

Cecil was a man
who said, "I like things clean!
But I don't want to work too hard,
so I'll make a **machine**."

He did some strange experiments
and tried to suck up dirt,
from pillows and on furniture
until his lips were hurt.

194

They both talk about things from the past.

Talk Together

Talk about what life was like before **machines**.
What is the difference between then and now?

Future Tense Verbs

Some **verbs** tell about actions that will happen in the future.

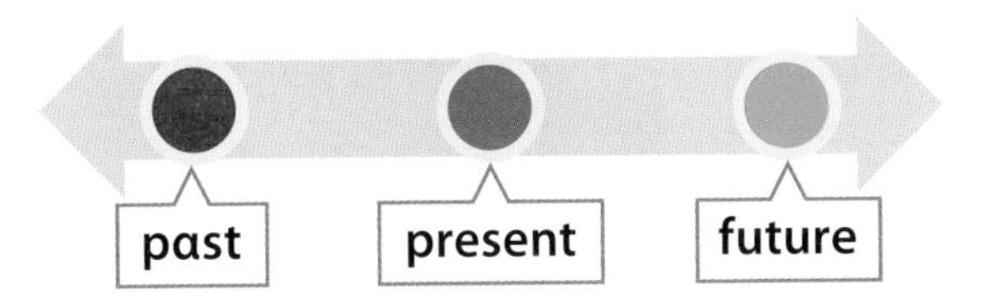

Grammar Rules Future Tense Verbs

To make verbs about the future:	
• Add **will** before the verb.	• He **will** invent.
Add these verbs after the subject and before the main verb: • I **am going to** • He/She/It **is going to** • They **are going to**	• He **is going to** make a machine.

Read a Sentence

Does this sentence tell about the future? Explain.

Cecil will make a new machine.

Write a Sentence 

Write a sentence about what machines will do in the future. Read it to a partner.

Write as a Friend

Write a Friendly Letter

What do you know about things from the past? Describe something old you have seen. Write a letter to a friend.

October 1

Dear Manny,

Last week, my dad showed me an old phone. The old phone did not have buttons. It had a dial with numbers. It had holes for your fingers.

The next day, I took the phone to school. We all dialed our phone numbers! I think old things are fun to use.

Your friend,

Altagracia

Write your friend's name in the **greeting**.

In the **body** of the letter, tell your news. This could include a **main idea** and details.

Write a **closing** and sign your name.

Language Frames

- The main idea is ____ .
- I think ____ .

❶ Plan and Write

Talk about things from the past with a partner. Draw a picture of one old thing. Write a list of details. Discuss your main idea. Tell your partner what you think about old things.

Write the main idea. Then write sentences with details. Remember to express your opinion.

❷ Check Your Work

Revise and edit your writing. Use this checklist.

Checklist

- ☑ Think about different words you can use. Can you use compound words, synonyms, or antonyms?
- ☑ Did you use past tense and future tense verbs correctly?
- ☑ Trade work with a partner. Check for words that sound alike. Does the word meaning make sense in the sentence?

❸ Finish and Share

Finish your letter. Make sure the greeting and other features of a letter are correct.

Read your letter to a friend. Share your opinions.

I think old things are too slow.

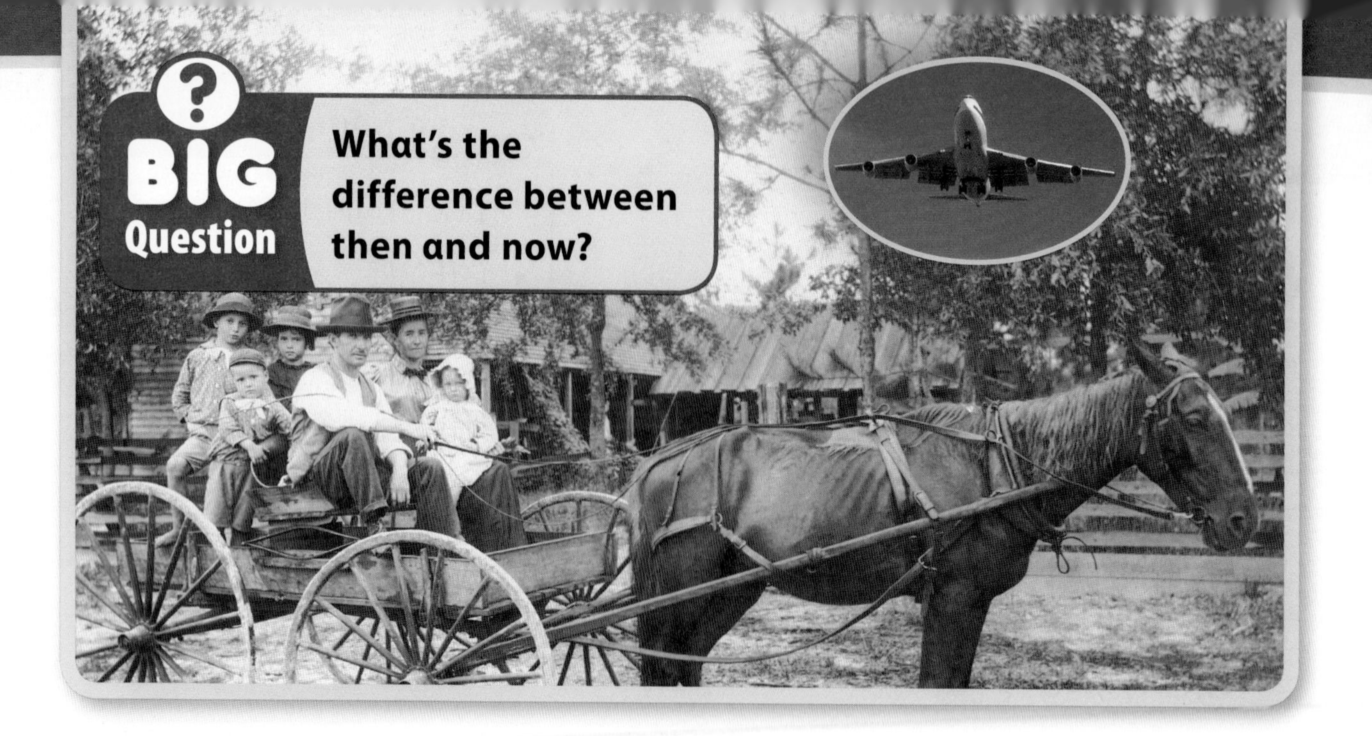

Share Your Ideas

Think about how we do things now and how we did things in the past. What's the difference between then and now? Choose one of these ways to share your ideas about the **Big Question**.

Write It!

Alphabetize a List

Write a list of all the **Key Words** from the unit. Then write the words again in alphabetical order. Alphabetize to the first or second letter. Use 3 of the words to write about things you learned about the past.

Talk About It!

Interview a Time Traveler

Pretend you are a time traveler. You are from the past. What is life like? What do you do? Have the group ask you questions. Then have another student pretend to be from the future. Ask more questions.

I am from the past. I walk to school. We don't have a bus.

Do It!

Make a Telephone

Have your teacher make a hole in the bottoms of two cans. Put one piece of string through both holes. Tie knots inside the cans to hold the string. Pull the cans apart until the string is tight. One partner listens while the other partner talks.

Get Out the Map!

BIG Question

Why do we need maps?

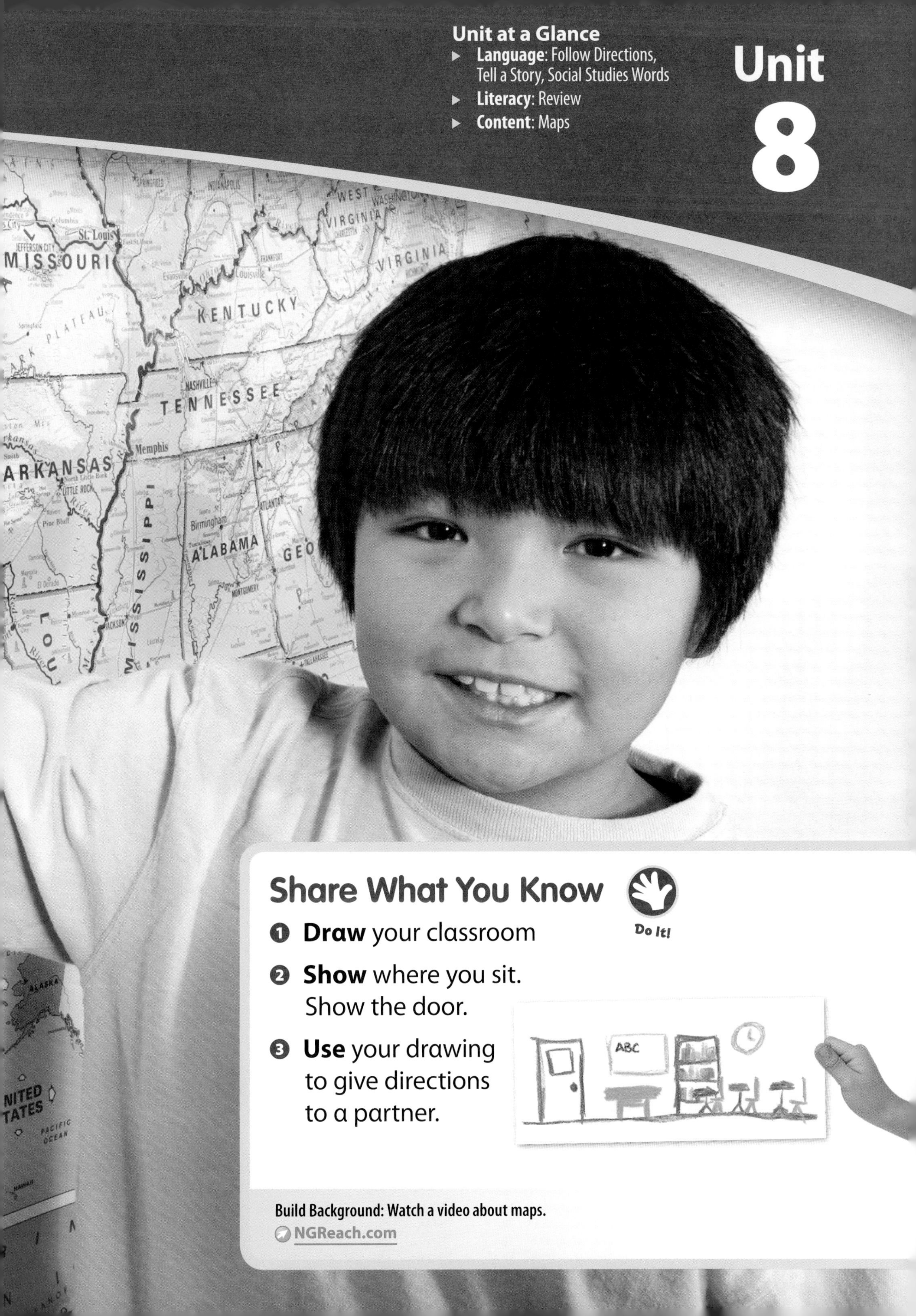

Unit 8

Unit at a Glance

- **Language**: Follow Directions, Tell a Story, Social Studies Words
- **Literacy**: Review
- **Content**: Maps

Share What You Know

Do It!

1. **Draw** your classroom
2. **Show** where you sit. Show the door.
3. **Use** your drawing to give directions to a partner.

Build Background: Watch a video about maps.
NGReach.com

High Frequency Words
- left
- right
- show
- turn

Follow Directions

Listen and sing. *Song* ((MP3)) 

At the Zoo

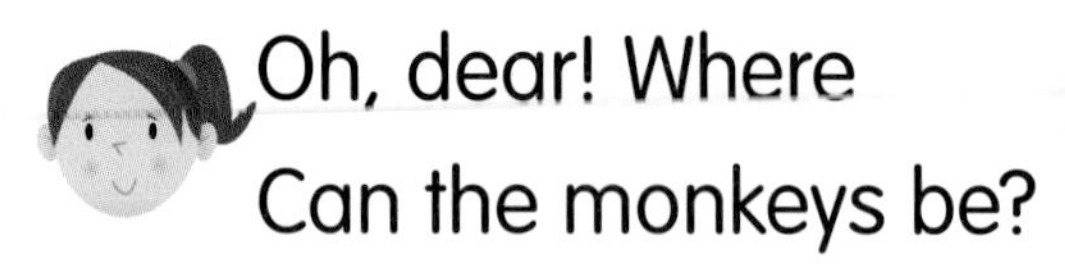

Oh, dear! Where
Can the monkeys be?

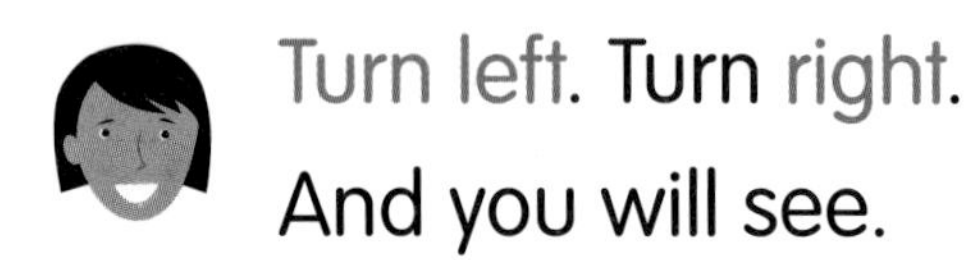

Turn left. Turn right.
And you will see.

Show me. Where
Can the monkeys be?

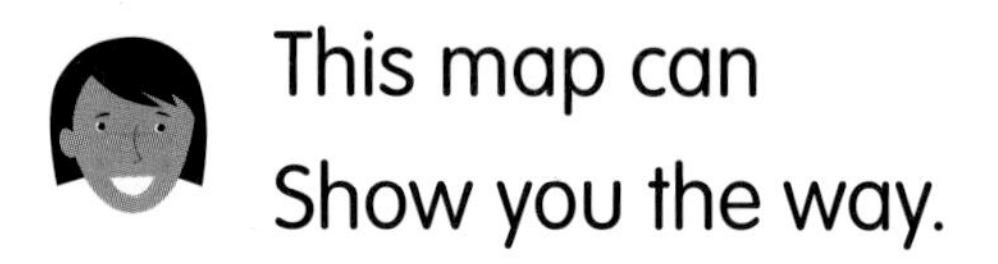

This map can
Show you the way.

Tune: "Oh, Dear, What Can the Matter Be?"

Key Words

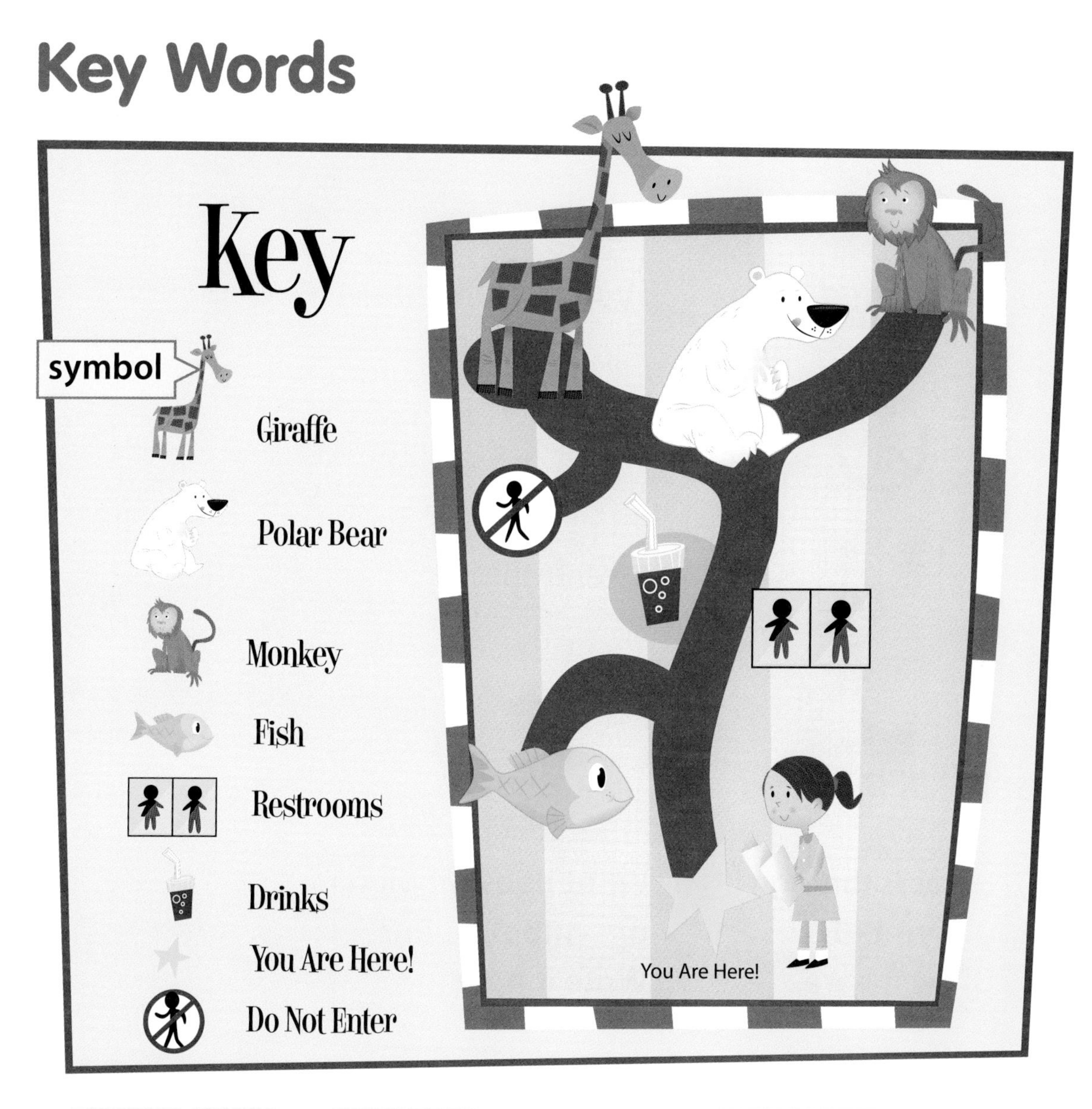

A **map key** is **useful**. It tells the **meaning** of a map's symbols. A symbol or sign can be a shape or a **picture**.

Talk Together

Tell a partner how to go from the entrance to see the fish. Use the map to help. Was the map useful?

Use Information

T Chart

Symbols and Signs	What It Means
	• do not enter
	• restrooms
	• giraffes

What is the sign or **symbol**? Draw it here.

What does the sign or symbol mean? Write it here.

Talk Together

Talk about the signs and symbols you see in your town. Draw two of them. Add them to the chart above.

More Key Words

• between

The house is **between** the two trees.

corner

Ashley Miller

I write my name in the **corner** of the paper.

distance

This man runs a long **distance**.

• show

I **show** my drawing.

sign

This **sign** means to add.

Talk Together

Use a **Key Word** to ask a question about maps.

What is the distance from your house to school?

Add words to My Vocabulary Notebook.
NGReach.com

• High Frequency Word

Read Informational Text

Informational text can explain something. This informational text explains how maps work.

Maps

Maps use **symbols**. Symbols are pictures or shapes that stand for real things.

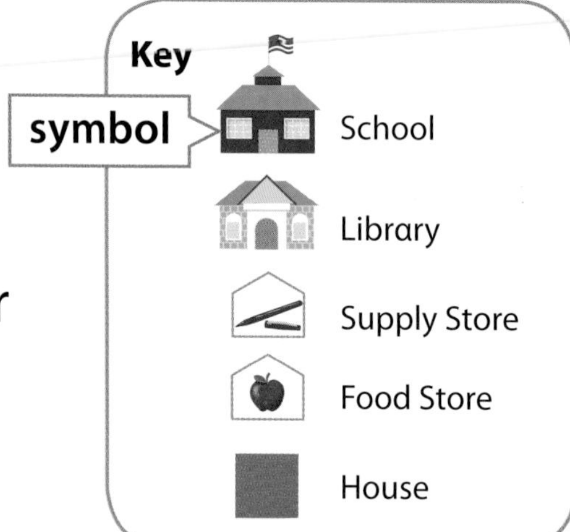

Reading Strategy

As you read, think of the 7 strategies you learned. Which strategies will help you understand the text?

If Maps Could Talk

by **Erika L. Shores**

illustrated by **Annie Bisset**

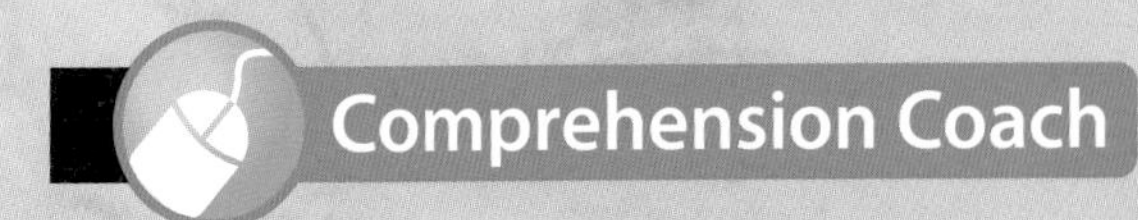

Maps: Finding Your Way

Where is the water slide? If you were a bird, you could fly up high to find it. But since you are not, you will have to use a **map**.

Maps use **symbols** to **show** where things are. The orange rectangle on the **Picture** Map is a symbol for the water slide. How do you know that? Read on.

Picture Map

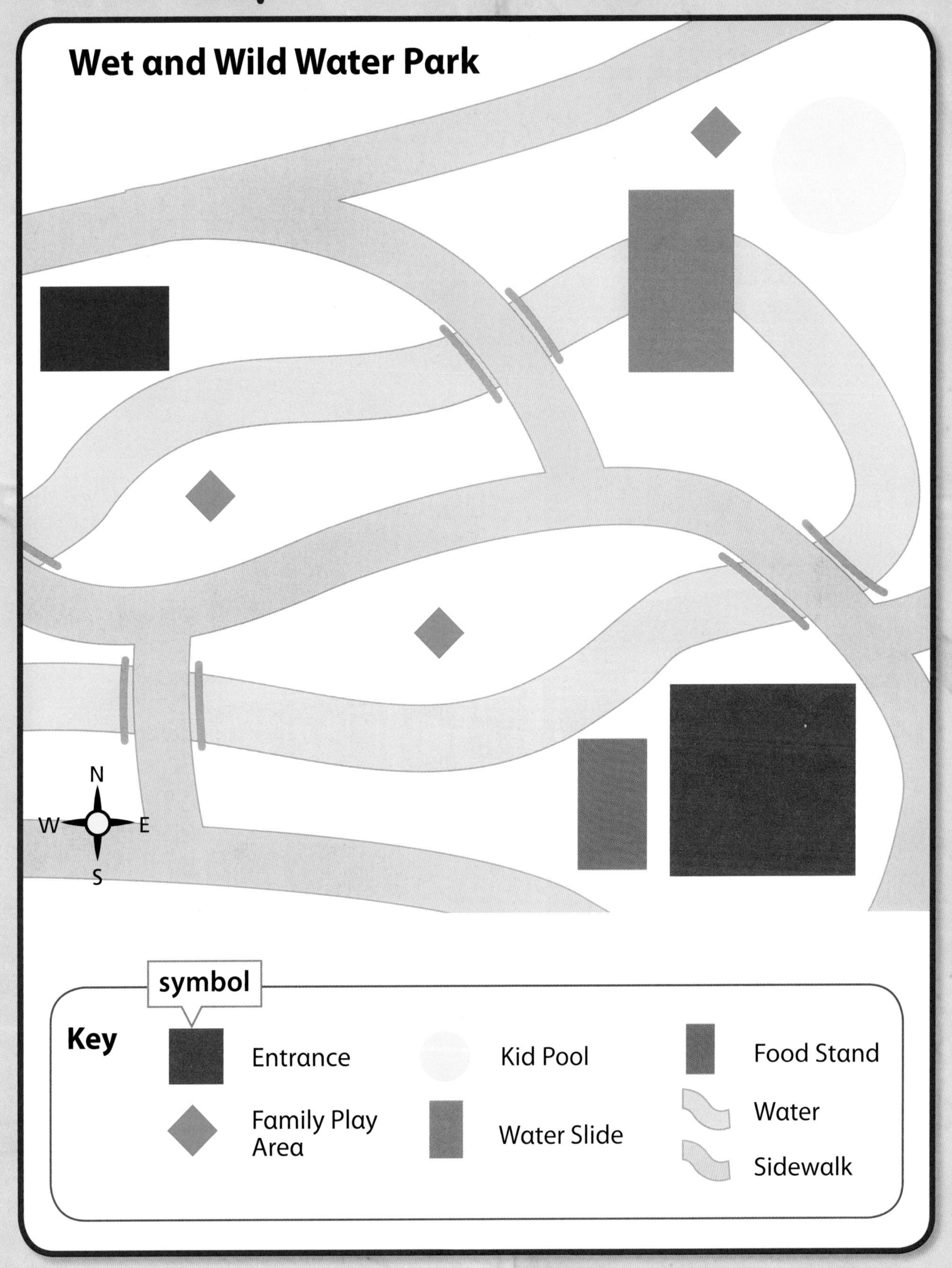

▲ **A picture map can use shapes or symbols to show where things are.**

The Key to Using Maps

The box at the bottom of a map is the **key**. Use the map key to learn the **meanings** of map symbols. Mapmakers use shapes to stand for real things. On the Street Map, what do the squares stand for?

Street Map

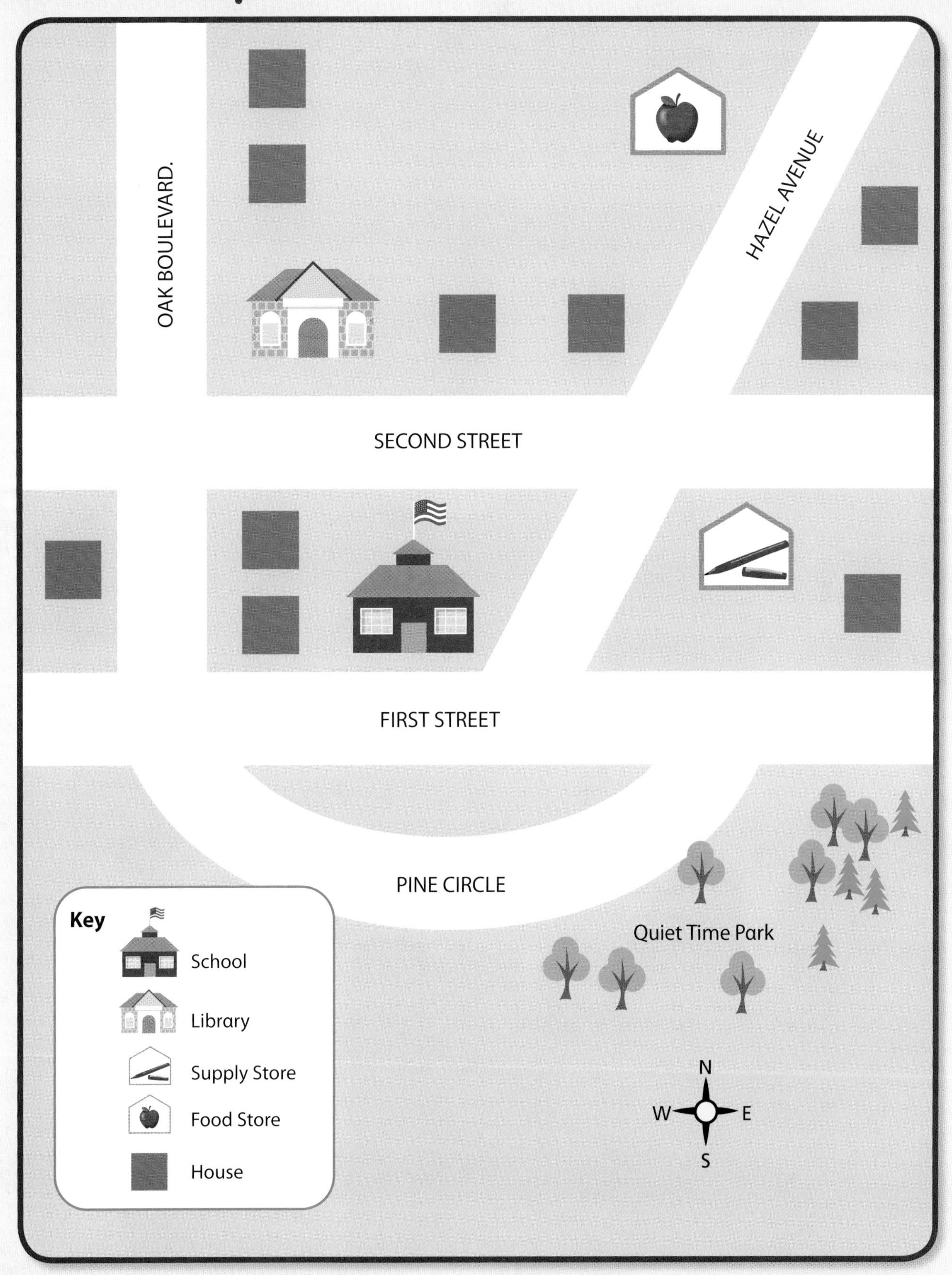

▲ **A street map shows street names and symbols to help people find their way around town.**

Symbols on the Road

Symbols on a road map help drivers find their way. A symbol shaped like a shield stands for a highway. Black circles stand for cities or towns.

Road Map

▲ A road map shows where roads and cities are.

Rain or Shine: Weather Symbols

What will the weather be like tomorrow? Look at a weather map in your city's newspaper.

Symbols on the Weather Map show the weather. Use the key to understand what the symbols mean.

Weather Map

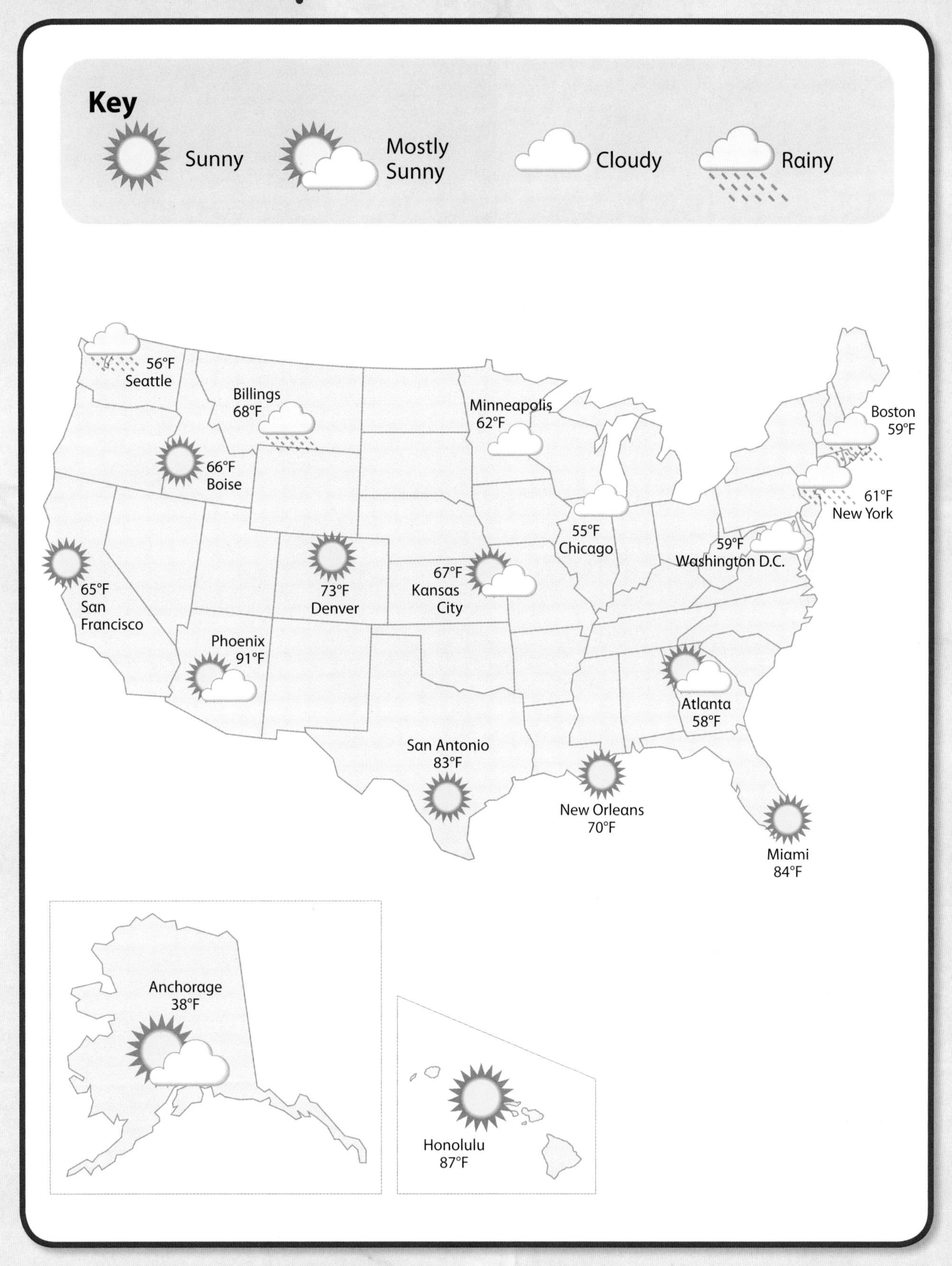

▲ **A weather map shows what the weather is like all around the country.**

No Key Needed: Picture Symbols

Most maps have a key. But there are some maps that don't have one. These maps use symbols that look like the real things they stand for.

Can you find the giraffes on this Picture Map?

Picture Map

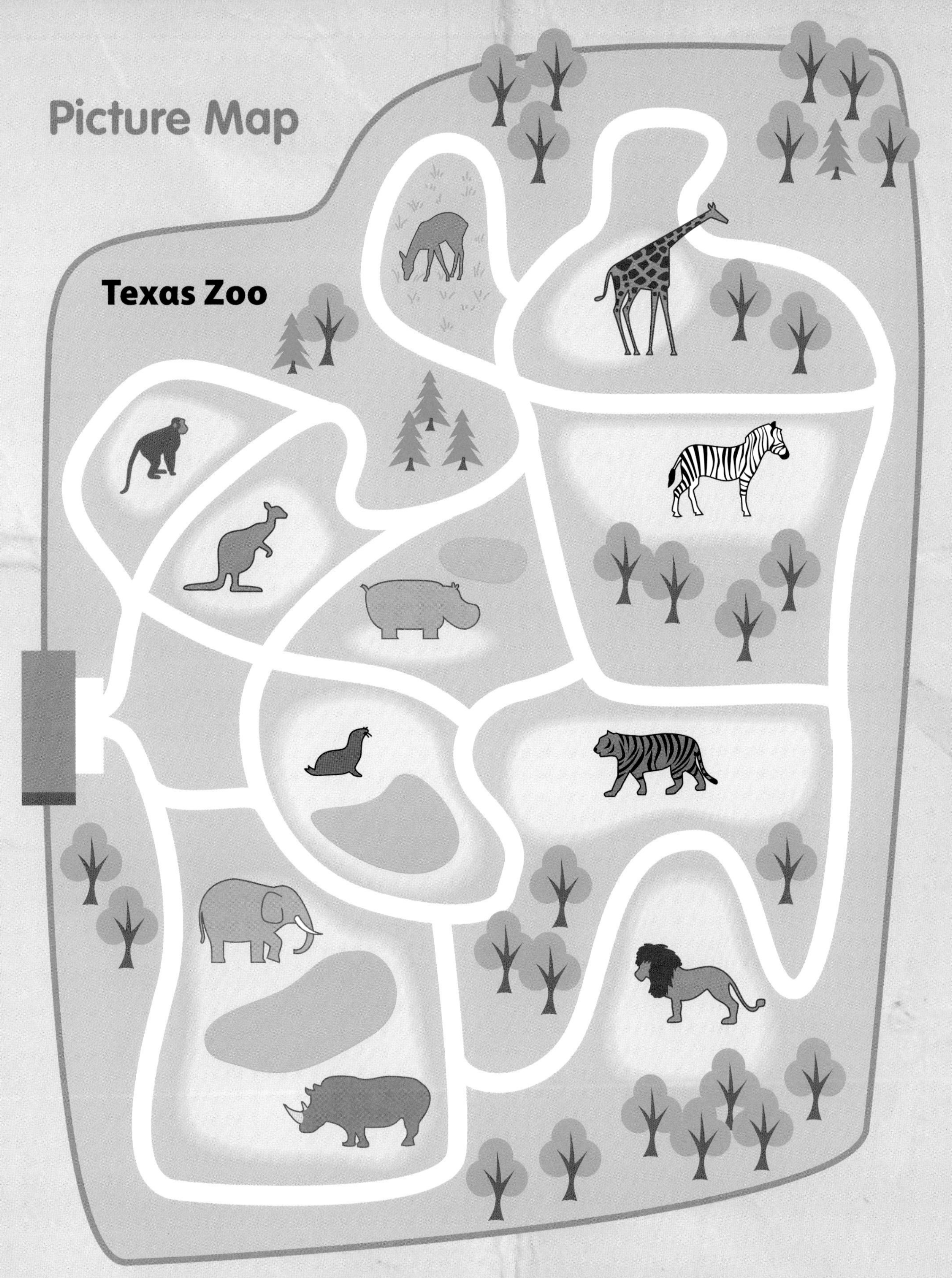

▲ This picture map uses picture symbols to show where to find the animals at the zoo.

Make Your Own Map

Use these steps to make your own map. Try to draw a map of your school.

Step 1

Draw the outline of your school. Show what your school would look like from above.

Step 2

Draw your classroom as a square. Put a symbol in the classroom, such as a star.

Step 3

Draw other rooms in your school, like the cafeteria. Add hallways, restrooms, and doors.

Step 4

Draw the library. Put a symbol in the library, such as an X.

Step 5

Make a key for your map. Draw and label the symbols for all the places you put on your map. ❖

Picture Map

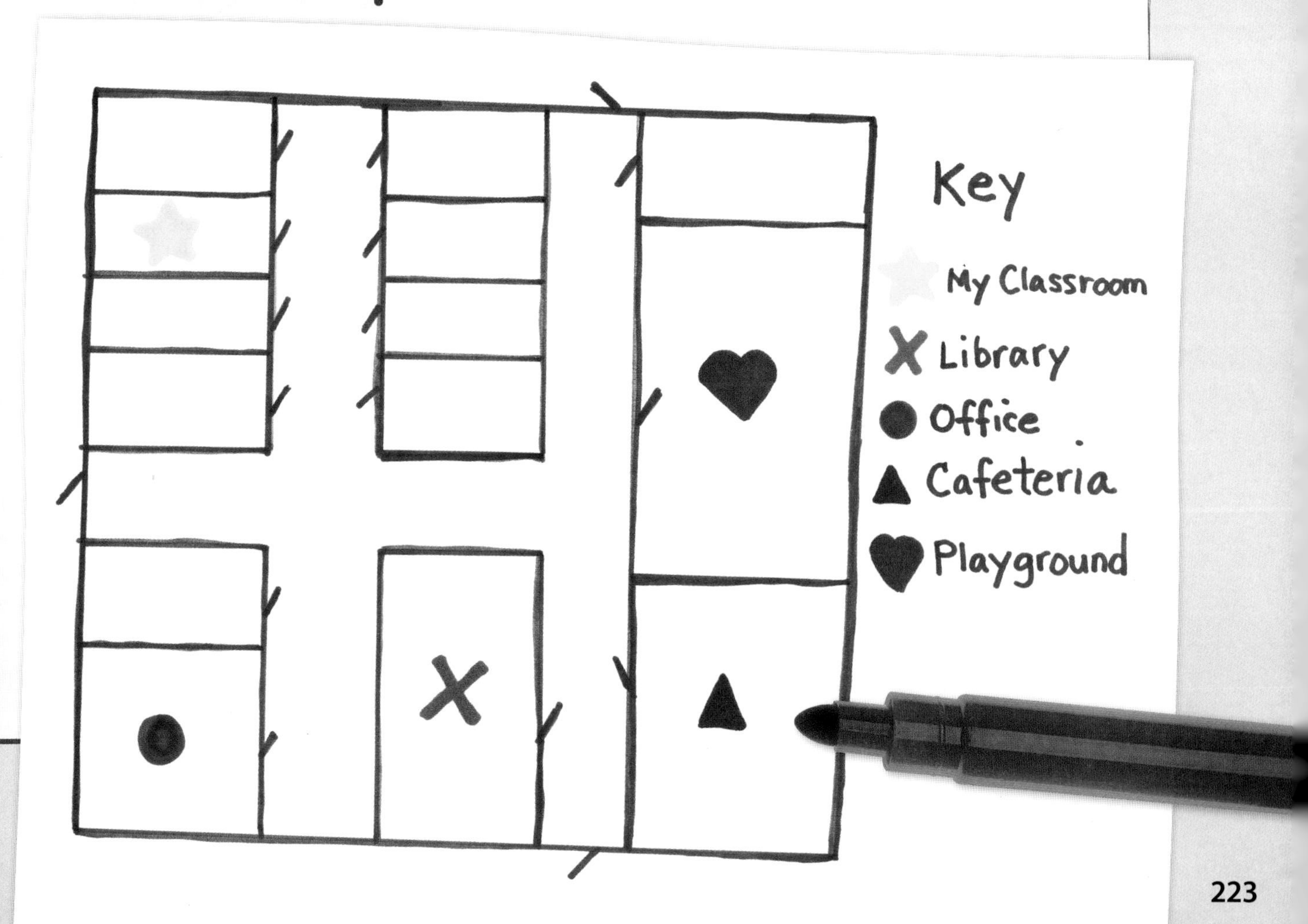

Talk About It 

1. What does a **map key show**?

A map key shows ____ .

2. Why do you need a key to understand most maps?

You need a key to understand ____ .

3. Why do people use road maps?

People use road maps to ____ .

Learn test-taking strategies.

NGReach.com

Write About It 

What did you learn from "If Maps Could Talk"? Write a comment.

I learned ____ from page ____ .

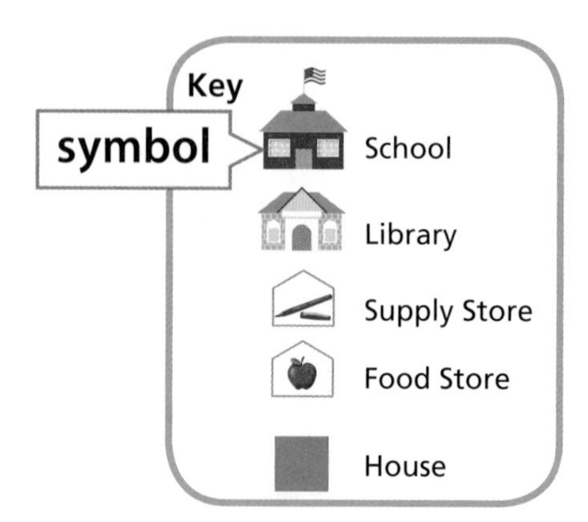

Use Information

What **signs** and symbols did you see in the text? What do they **mean**?

T Chart

Symbols and Signs	What It Means
	• mostly sunny • •

Use your chart. Tell a partner what you learned about signs, symbols, and maps.

A symbol can be a picture of a real thing.

Suffixes

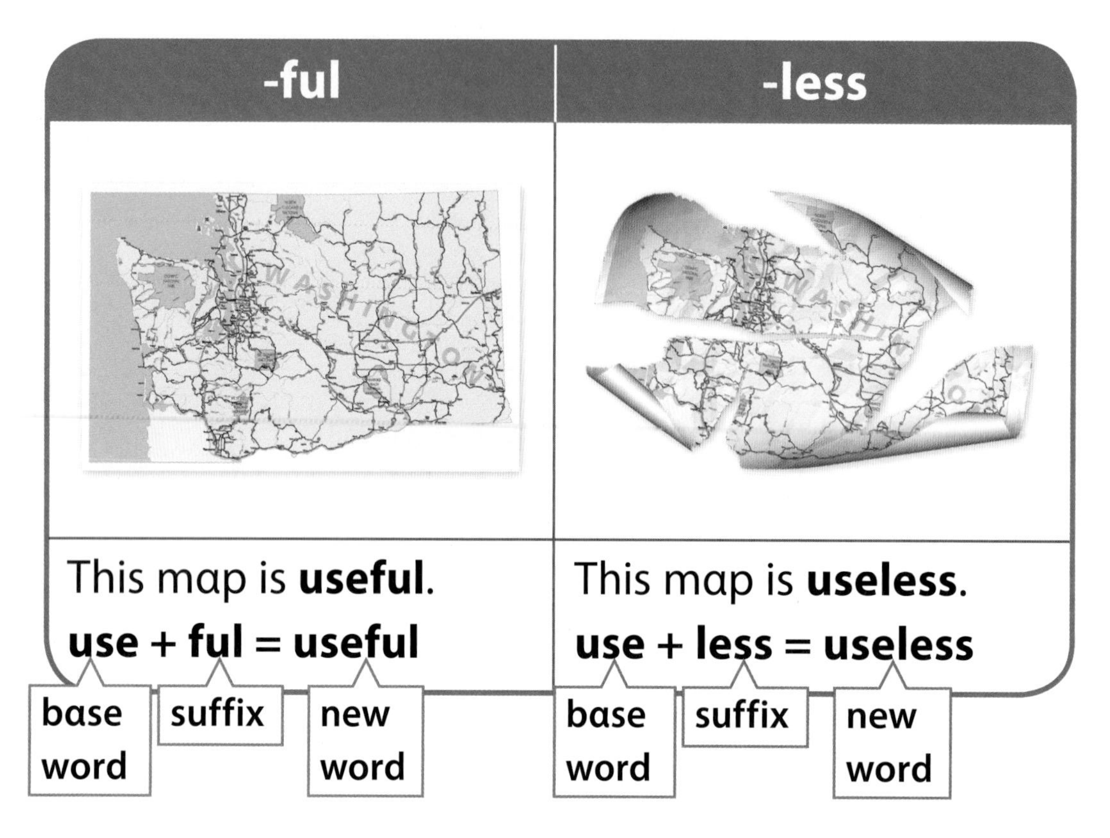

-ful
-less
This map is **useful**.
use + ful = useful
base word
suffix
new word
This map is **useless**.
use + less = useless
base word
suffix
new word

Sometimes you can add a **suffix**, like **–ful** or **–less**, to the end of a word to make a new word. What do **useful** and **useless** mean?

Try It Together

Add **-ful** and **-less** to each word. How do the meanings change?

Word	-ful	-less
care	careful	careless
help		
hope		

Connect Across Texts Read more about how **maps** and directions lead us to interesting places.

Genre A **poem** uses words to create images in your mind.

Haiku

By Richard Wright

Keep straight down this block
Then turn right where you will find
A peach tree blooming

Compare Genres

How are the words in "If Maps Could Talk" and "Haiku" different?

Informational Text

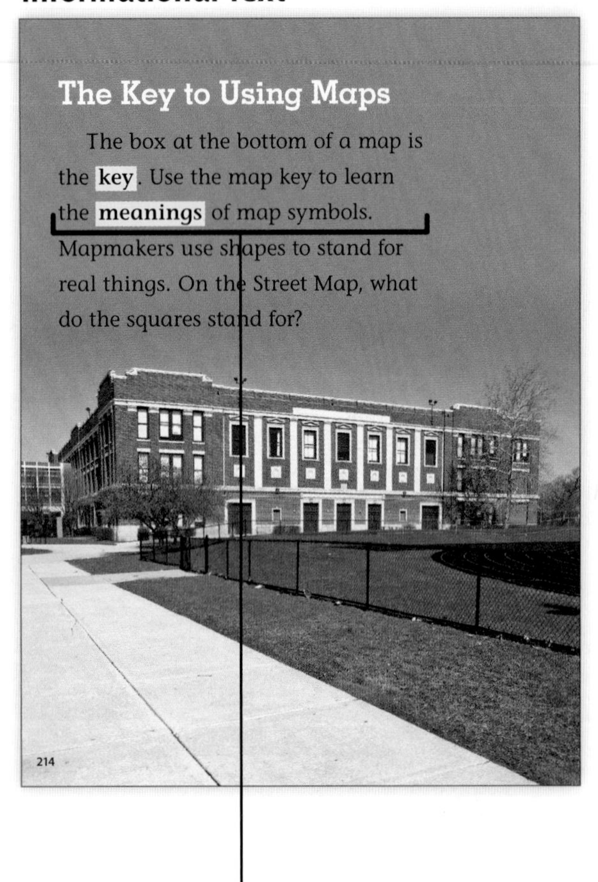
The Key to Using Maps

The box at the bottom of a map is the key. Use the map key to learn the meanings of map symbols. Mapmakers use shapes to stand for real things. On the Street Map, what do the squares stand for?

214

The text gives definitions.

Poem

Keep straight down this block
Then turn right where you will find
A peach tree blooming

228

The words create images in your mind.

Talk Together

Think about what you read and learned. Why do we need maps?

Adverbs

An **adverb** can tell more about a **verb**.

We **stand** **quietly** by the peach tree.

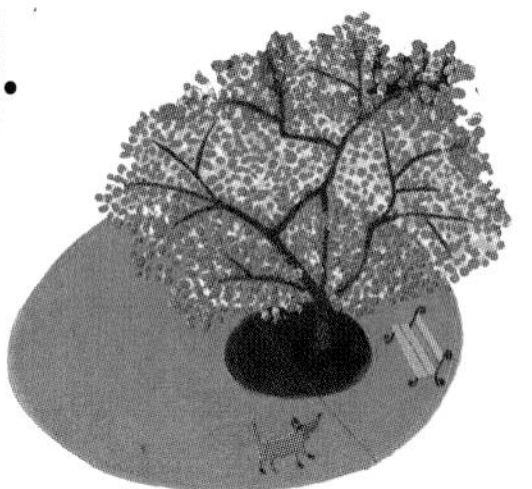

Grammar Rules Adverbs

Adverbs can tell:	Examples
• **how** something happens. These adverbs often end in -**ly**.	They **walk** **slowly**.
• **where** something happens.	The peach tree **is** **north** of the bench.
• **when** something happens.	We **always** **visit** the peach tree.

Read a Sentence

Which word is an adverb? How do you know?

The flower petals fall softly from the tree.

Write a Sentence 

Write a sentence to tell how you got ready for school today. Use an adverb.

High Frequency Words
once
story
tell

Tell a Story

Listen and chant. *Chant* MP3

A story has a problem,
A solution as well.
Here is an example
Of a story to tell.

Once upon a time,
A boy named Jack.
Went on a hike
And lost his way back.

He looked to the east.
He looked to the west.
He looked for the path
That was the best.

He looked up and down,
And then . . . hooray!
He looked on a map
And found his way.

Key Words

Talk Together

Use the map to tell a story.

Identify Problem and Solution

Problem-and-Solution Chart

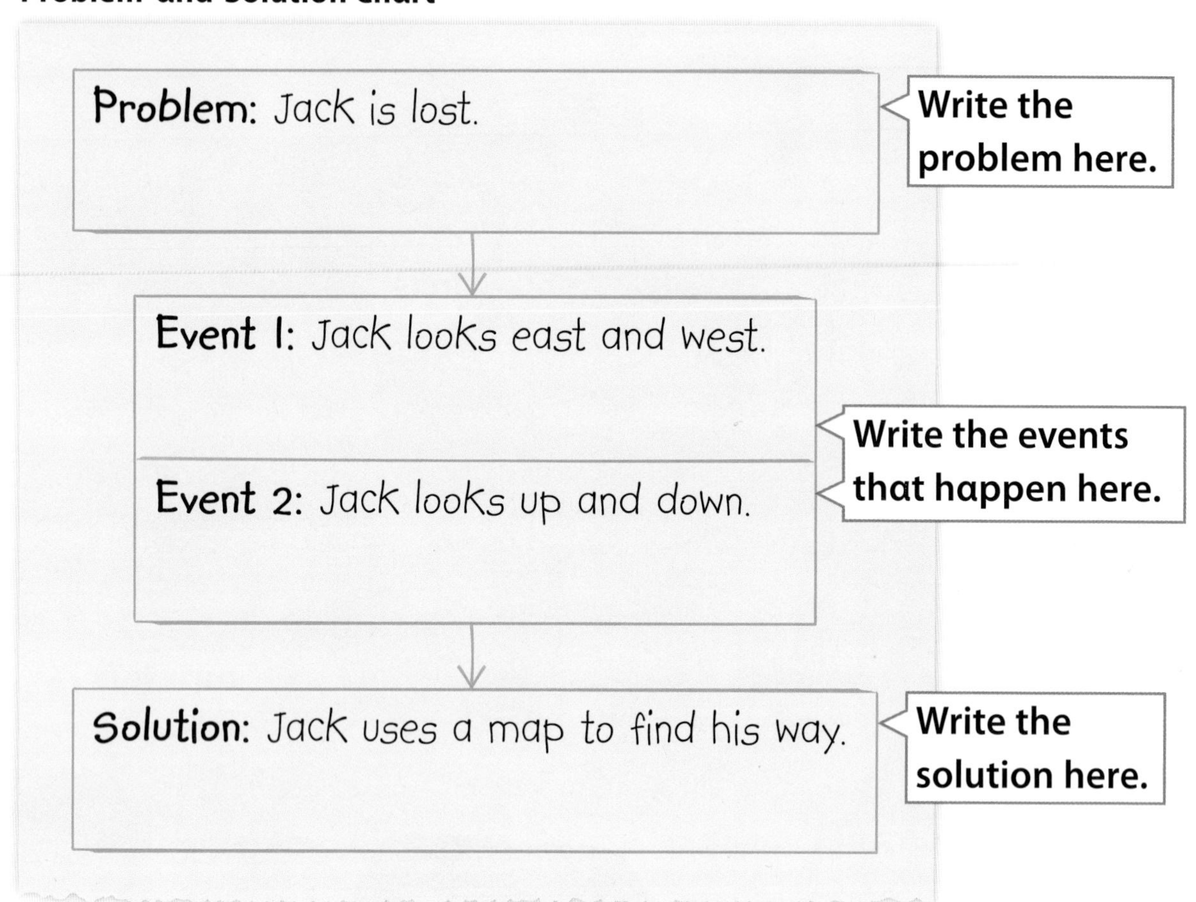

Problem: Jack is lost.
Write the problem here.
Event 1: Jack looks east and west.
Event 2: Jack looks up and down.
Write the events that happen here.
Solution: Jack uses a map to find his way.
Write the solution here.

Look for problems and solutions as you listen or read.

Talk Together

Tell a different story. Imagine Jack is with a friend. Make a problem-and-solution chart.

More Key Words

direction

North is a **direction**.

• **far**

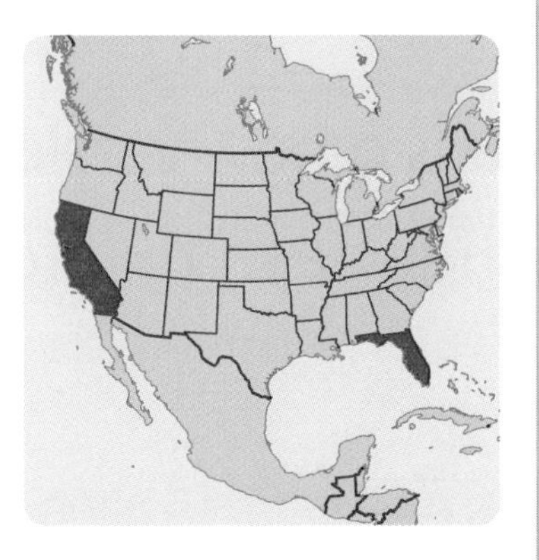

The red states are **far** from each other.

• **follow**

Follow the path through the grass.

location

Our tent is in a good **location** by the lake.

• **near**

I sit **near** the window.

• High Frequency Word

Talk Together

Describe a **Key Word** while your partner asks questions about it.

There are four of them. One of them is South.

Is it direction?

Add words to My Vocabulary Notebook.
NGReach.com

Read a Modern Fairy Tale

A **modern fairy tale** is a new version of an old story that has been told for many years.

Most fairy tales begin like this.

Once upon a time, a young girl lived in a village south of a forest.

Reading Strategy

As you read, think of the 7 strategies you learned. Which strategies will help you understand the text?

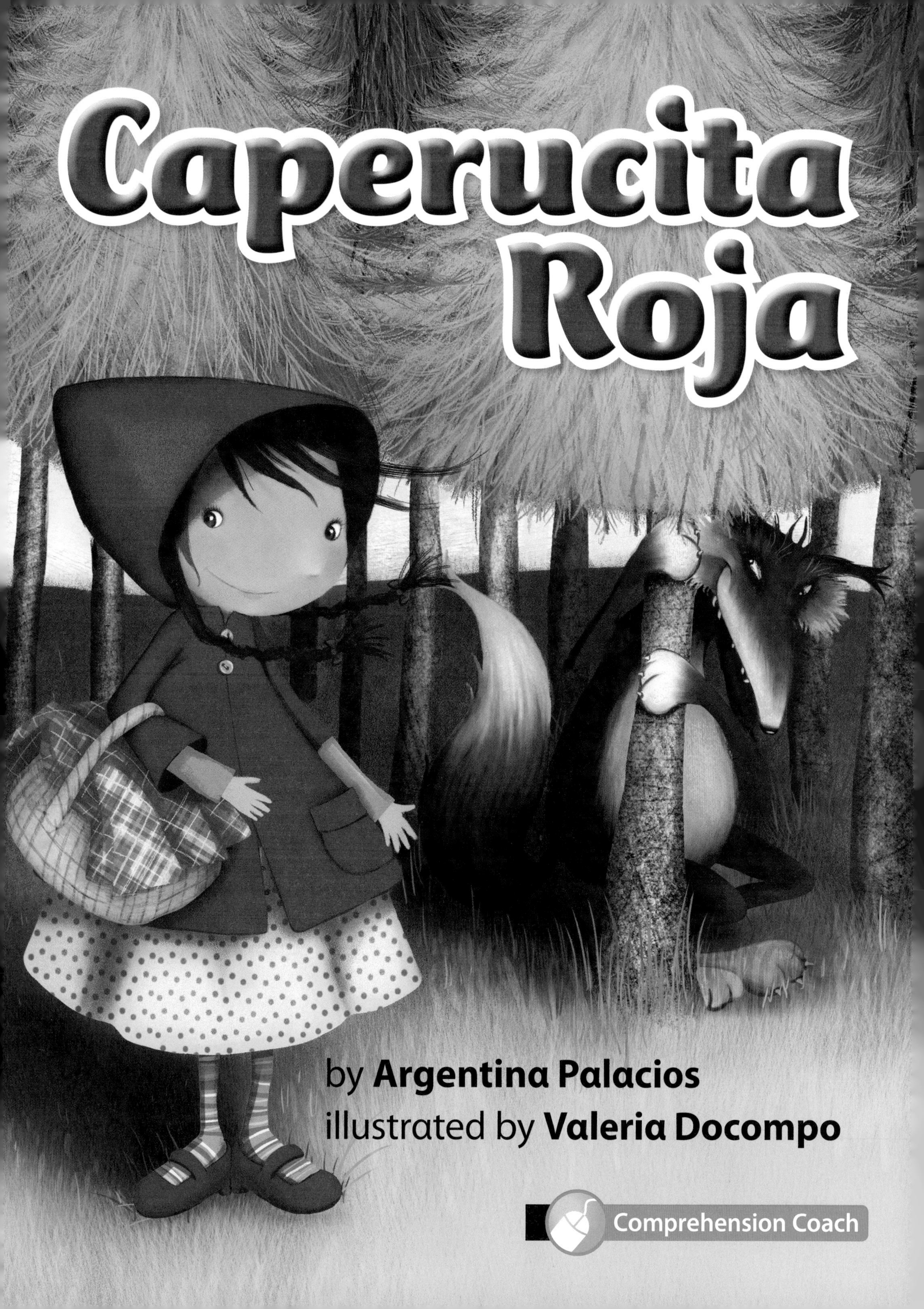
Caperucita Roja
by Argentina Palacios
illustrated by Valeria Docompo
Comprehension Coach

Once upon a time, a young girl lived in a village **south** of a forest. She had a red riding hood. She loved it. She wore her red riding hood every day. So people called her Caperucita Roja.

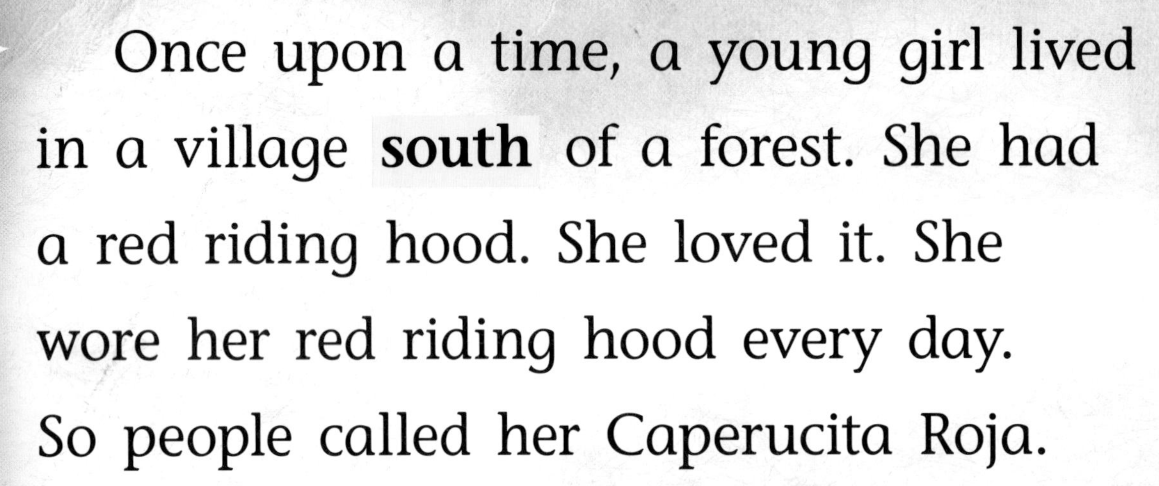

One day, Caperucita Roja's Mamá said, "Hija, Abuelita is sick. Take her some food. Visit with her for a while."

"Sí, Mamá," Caperucita Roja said. "I will go now."

"**Follow** the shortest **path**. Do not get distracted. Go quickly!" Mamá said. "Do not forget your map."

"Sí, Mamá. I will take the map with me," said Caperucita Roja.

The village was south of the forest. Abuelita's house was **north** of the forest. Caperucita Roja followed the **directions** on her map. She knew exactly where to go!

Suddenly, a wolf stepped out of the forest. He was big, and he was bad. So people called him Big Bad Wolf.

"Hello, Caperucita Roja," he said. "Look at those pretty flowers. You should take some flowers to Abuelita."

One, two, three, four flowers. Caperucita Roja got distracted.

The wolf wanted to eat Caperucita Roja. But people were walking on the path. They would not want Caperucita Roja to be eaten. They would stop him.

Big Bad Wolf was unhappy. Then he had an idea.

He ran away, but Caperucita Roja didn't notice. She was too busy picking flowers for Abuelita.

Big Bad Wolf thought he could get to Abuelita's house before Caperucita Roja. He checked his map to see what path he could take.

He ran to the **west**. Then he ran to the north. Then he ran a little to the **east**.

ABUELITA'S HOUSE
FARMER'S HOUSE
FOREST
CAPERUCITA ROJA'S HOUSE
LAGE

Big Bad Wolf knocked on Abuelita's door. "It is Caperucita Roja," he said.

"Come in, my dear," said Abuelita.

The wolf looked at Abuelita. He didn't want to eat her at all. She was too skinny.

"She does not look tasty," Big Bad Wolf said to himself. So he pushed Abuelita out of the bed and into the closet!

Then Big Bad Wolf put on one of Abuelita's nightgowns. "Now I look like Abuelita. I will eat Caperucita Roja," he said to himself.

Caperucita Roja knocked on the door.

"Come in!" Big Bad Wolf tried to sound like Abuelita. But his voice was too low.

"That does not sound like Abuelita," Caperucita Roja said to herself. She opened the door. Something was wrong.

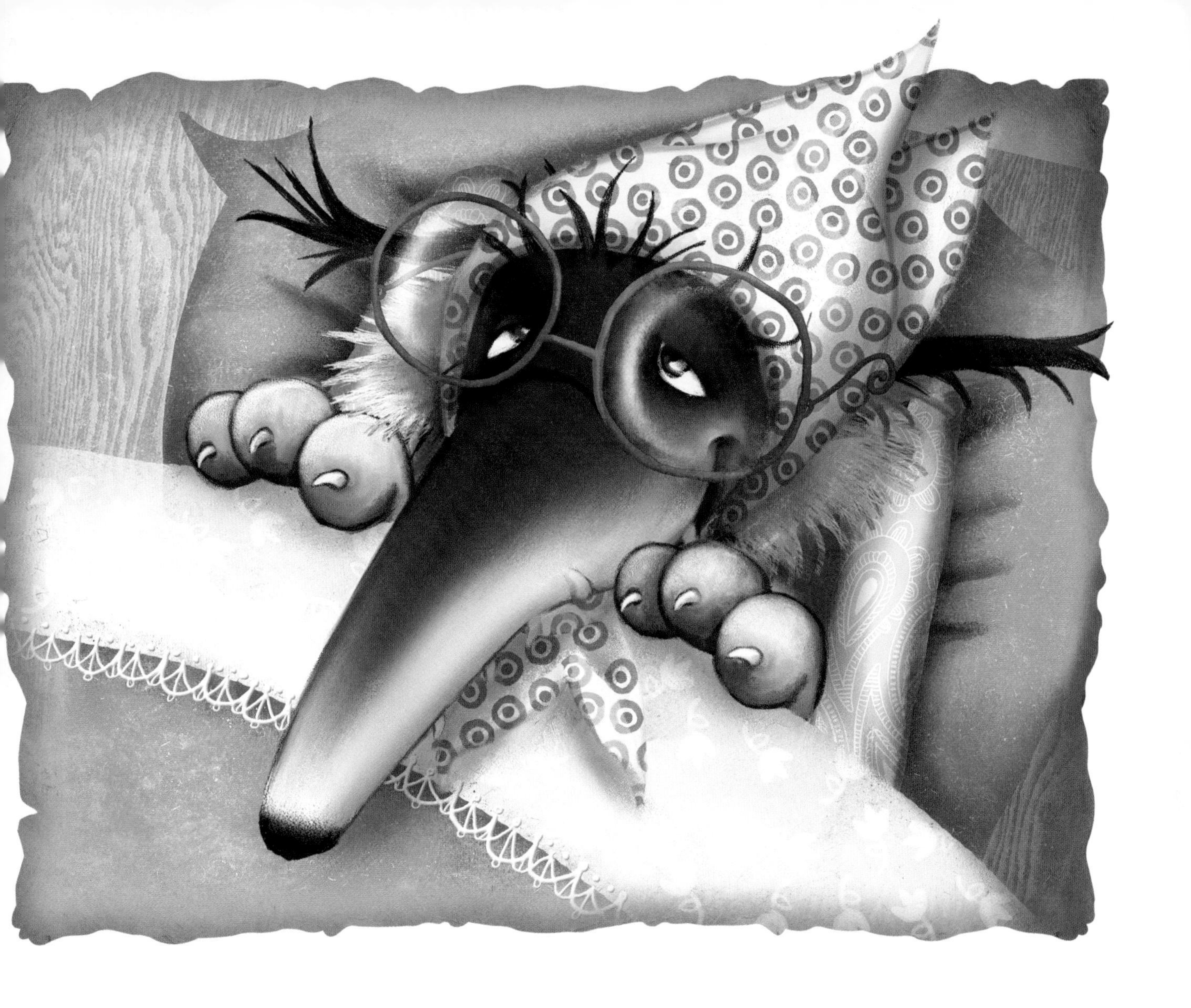

Caperucita Roja saw two long ears. They were not Abuelita's ears.

Then she saw one very long nose. It was not Abuelita's nose.

She saw two little, brown eyes. They were not Abuelita's eyes.

Caperucita Roja thought fast. "Who can help me? The farmer can! I will go get the farmer!"

Caperucita Roja looked at her map. It showed where the farmer lived.

Caperucita Roja went east. She ran and ran. She told the farmer about the wolf.

"I scare rabbits out of my garden every day. I will scare away that wolf! I will save Abuelita!" he shouted. And they ran off together.

When Big Bad Wolf saw the angry farmer, he jumped out of the bed. He tried to go **right**. He tried to go **left**. He could not escape. The farmer was too fast for him. So Big Bad Wolf jumped out of the window!

Caperucita Roja opened the closet door. She helped Abuelita back into the bed.

"Thank you for your help!" Caperucita Roja said to the farmer. "I could not have saved Abuelita without you."

Abuelita began to feel better quickly. She and the farmer became good friends. They never saw Big Bad Wolf again.

Caperucita Roja often came to visit Abuelita and the farmer. And they all lived happily ever after. ❖

AWARD WINNER

Meet the Author

Argentina Palacios

Argentina Palacios was born in Panama, and then moved to the United States. She was a Spanish teacher in Texas.

Now Ms. Palacios writes stories in English and Spanish. She also gives tours to children at a zoo because she loves animals.

◀ **Argentina Palacios**

Writer's Craft

Argentina Palacios ended this story by solving the problem and telling us what happens to the characters afterward. What else would you add to the ending?

Talk About It

1. Which character in the story is sick?

   ____ is sick.

2. How does Big Bad Wolf get to Abuelita's house before Caperucita Roja?

   Big Bad Wolf ____ .

3. How does Caperucita Roja use a map to get help?

   Caperucita Roja uses a map to ____ .

Learn test-taking strategies.
NGReach.com

Write About It

This fairy tale teaches you to know when you are in trouble and to go for help. When have you needed help? Who did you go to?

I needed help ____ .
I went to ____ .

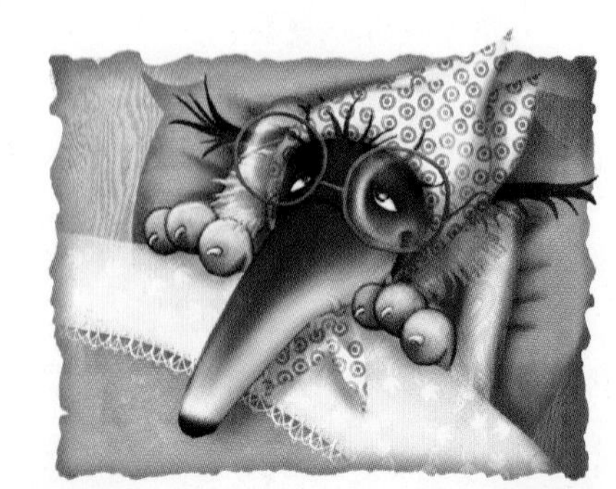

Identify Problem and Solution

Caperucita Roja has a problem with the Big Bad Wolf. What is it and how does she solve it?

Problem-and-Solution Chart

Problem: Big Bad Wolf is trying to eat Caperucita Roja.

Event 1:

Event 2:

Event 3:

Solution:

Use your chart to retell the story of *Caperucita Roja*.

The farmer scares Big Bad Wolf away.

Prefixes

base word
un-
Caperucita is **happy**.
happy
base word
Big Bad Wolf is **unhappy**.
un + happy = unhappy
prefix
base word
new word

A **prefix** is a word part. Add a prefix to the **beginning** of a base word to change the meaning. What does **unhappy** mean?

Try It Together

Add the prefix **un**- to each word. Talk about the new meaning of each word.

Word	New Word
lucky	unlucky
safe	
kind	
fair	

Connect Across Texts Learn more about what helps us use maps.

Genre A **how-to article** teaches you how to do something.

How to Make a Compass

by Michael A. DiSpezio

A compass is a tool that can tell which **direction** you are going. There are four main directions: **North**, **South**, **East**, and **West**.

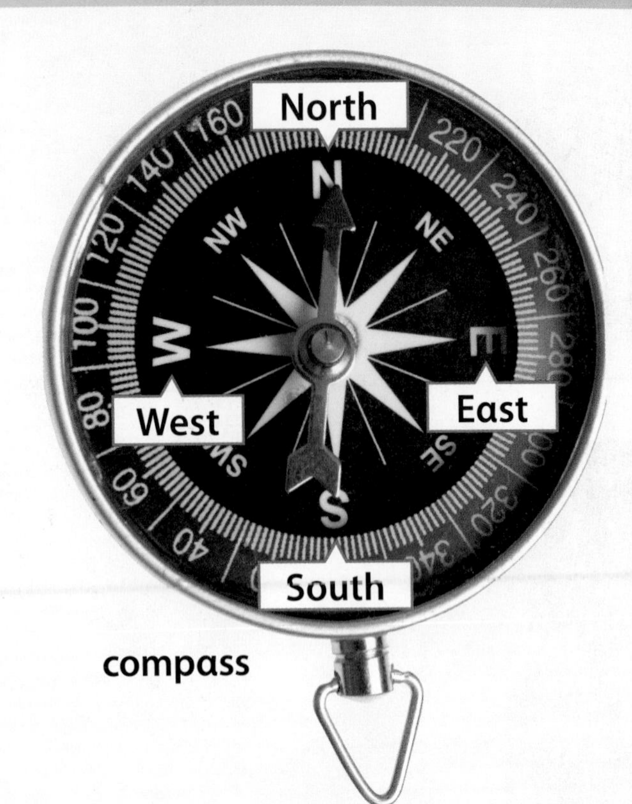

compass

Materials

sewing needle

clear container

water

bar magnet

plastic foam cup

paper

crayons

scissors

Step 1

Cut out the bottom of the foam cup so you have a flat circle.

Step 2

Magnetize the needle. Rub it the same direction on the bar magnet 20 times.

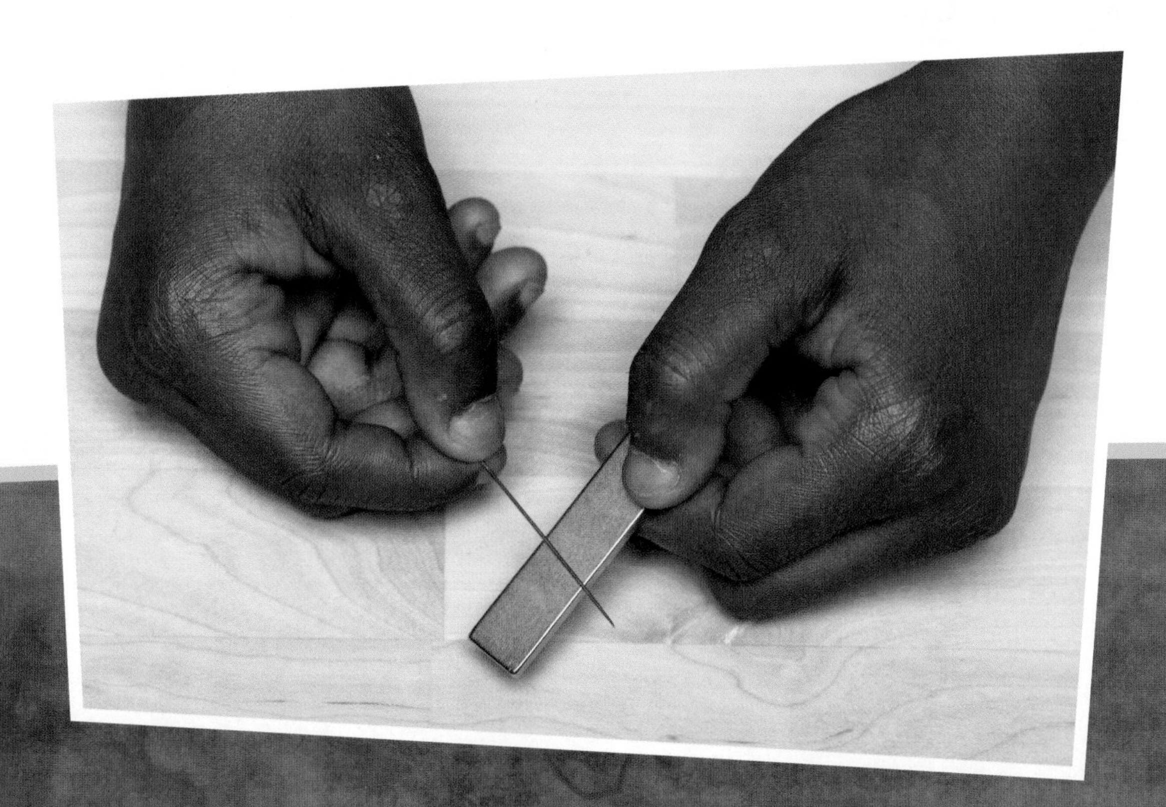

Step 3

Lay the needle on the foam circle.

Step 4

Put the foam and the needle in the water. The needle will stop moving when it points North.

Step 5

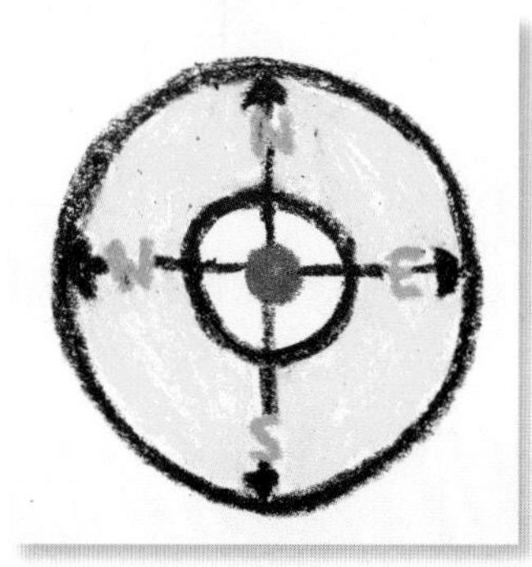

Draw a compass rose like this one.

Fill the clear container with water. Place it over your compass rose.

Step 6

Move the paper around until the needle lines up with the N on the compass rose.

Think of all the places north of you. Which places are south of you?

Compare Genres

How are the purposes of a fairy tale like *Caperucita Roja* and a How-to Article like "How to Make a Compass" different?

Fairy Tale

Suddenly, a wolf stepped out of the forest. He was big, and he was bad. So people called him Big Bad Wolf.
"Hello, Caperucita Roja," he said. "Look at those pretty flowers. You should take some flowers to Abuelita."
243

Tells a story that cannot happen in real life.

How-to Article

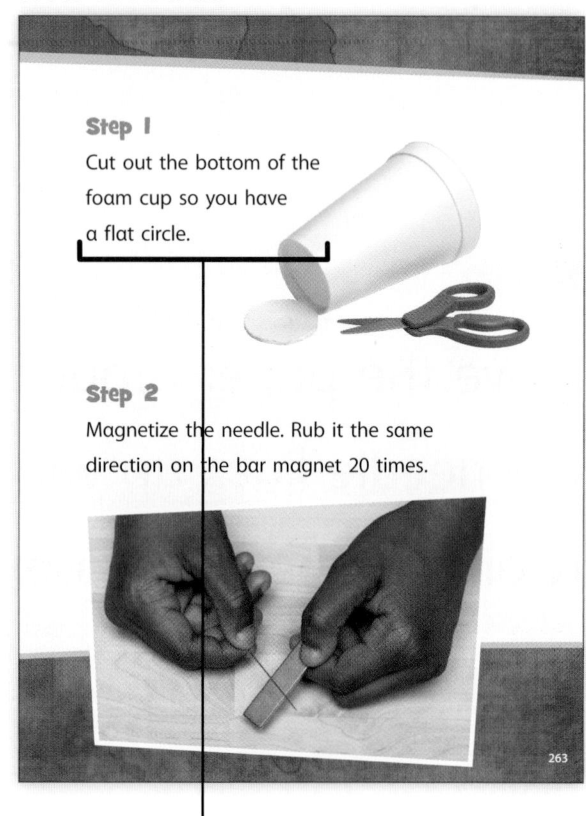

Step 1
Cut out the bottom of the foam cup so you have a flat circle.
Step 2
Magnetize the needle. Rub it the same direction on the bar magnet 20 times.
263

Tells how to make something that is real.

Talk Together

Think about what you read and learned. Why do we need maps?

Prepositions

Prepositions tell where something is.

The needle is **on** the foam.

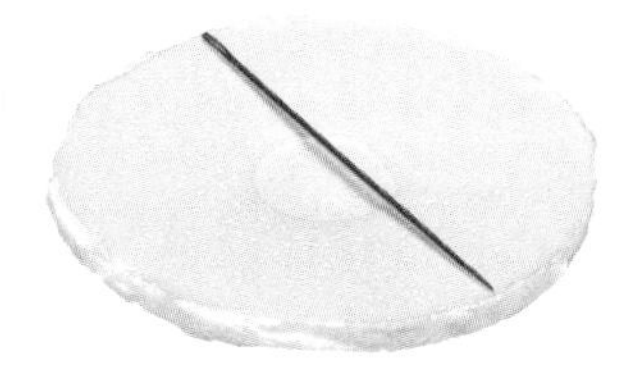

The compass is **next to** the map.

Prepositions tell where. Put prepositions before the noun that names a place.	The compass is **on** the **table**. (**on** = preposition; **table** = noun that names a place)

Read a Sentence

Draw what the sentence tells. Use your drawing to tell a partner what the preposition means.

The compass rose is **under** the glass.

Write a Sentence

Write a sentence that tells where you find scissors in your classroom. Use a preposition. Read it to a partner.

Write as a Reader

Write Literary Response

Think about a story. What was the problem and solution? What did you like about it? Write a response for a partner.

Caperucita Roja

by Aziza Noor

Tell the title of the story.

I read Caperucita Roja. **Caperucita Roja had to save Abuelita from the wolf**.

problem

Tell what the story is about.

Caperucita Roja ran to get the farmer. **The helpful farmer scared the wolf away.**

solution

They all lived happily ever after. I think this happy ending makes Caperucita Roja a good story.

Tell what you liked about the story.

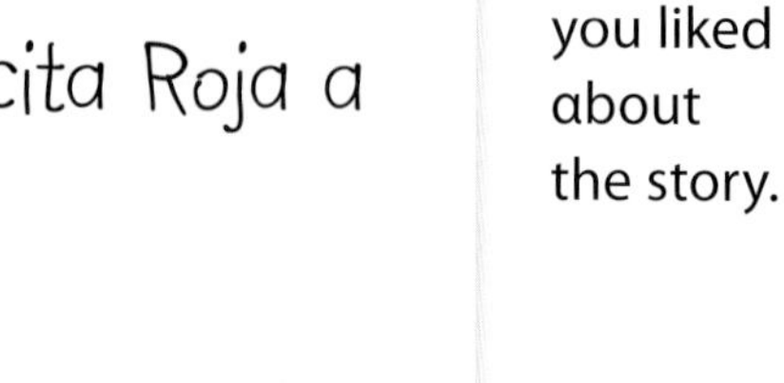

❶ Plan and Write

Language Frames

- The problem was ___.
- The solution was ___.

Talk with a partner about stories you have read. Pick one story you like. Talk about how the author tells the story. Tell your partner the story's problem and solution.

Write the problem and solution. Then write what makes the story good.

❷ Check Your Work

Revise and edit your writing. Use this checklist.

Checklist

- ☑ Does the story you reviewed have a strong ending?
- ☑ Can you add any prefixes or suffixes?
- ☑ Check your sentences. Did you use prepositions correctly?
- ☑ Check for different ways to spell sounds you know. Circle words to check. Correct spelling errors.

❸ Finish and Share

Finish your response. Write each sentence neatly. Begin a new paragraph when you change ideas.

Read your response clearly. Listen carefully to your partner. Then ask questions. Share what you know.

Why was the ending your favorite part of Caperucita Roja?

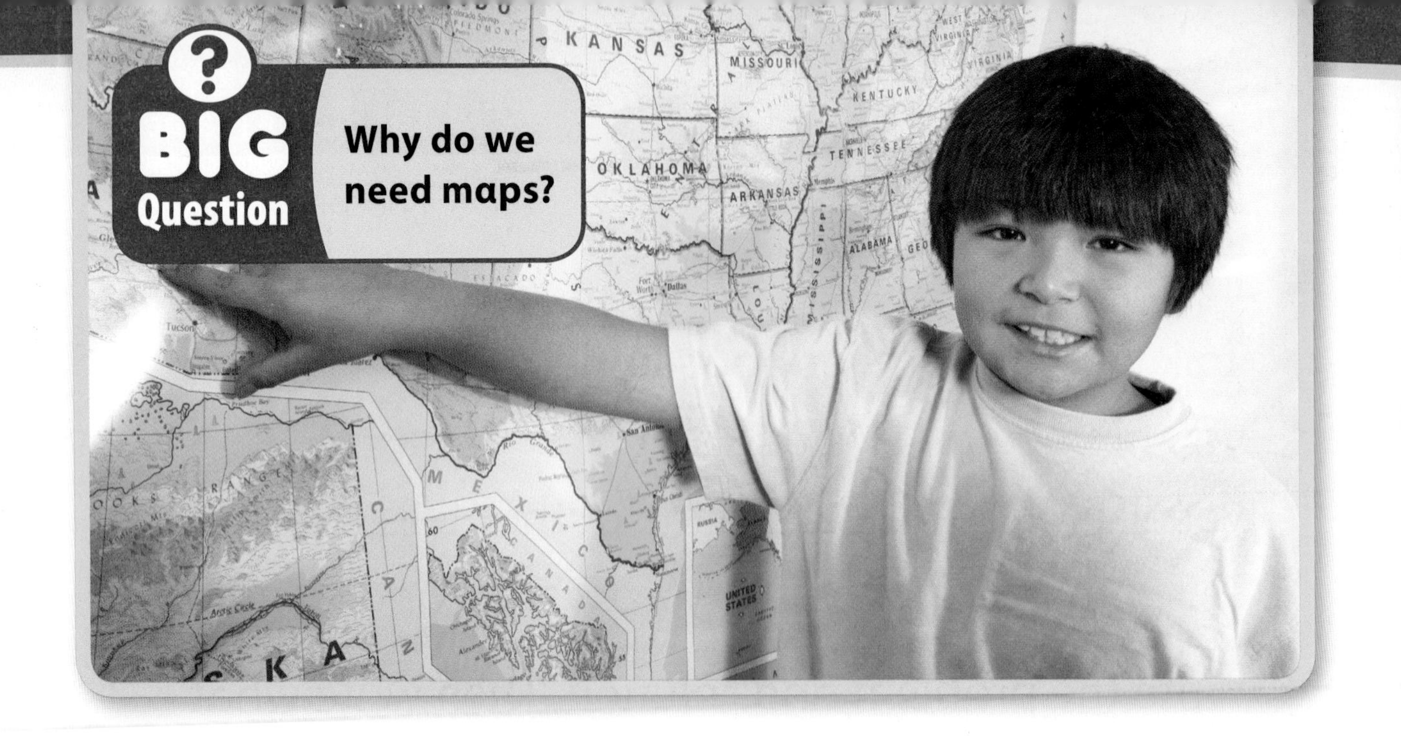

Share Your Ideas

Think about what maps show us. Why do we need maps? Choose one of these ways to share your ideas about the **Big Question**.

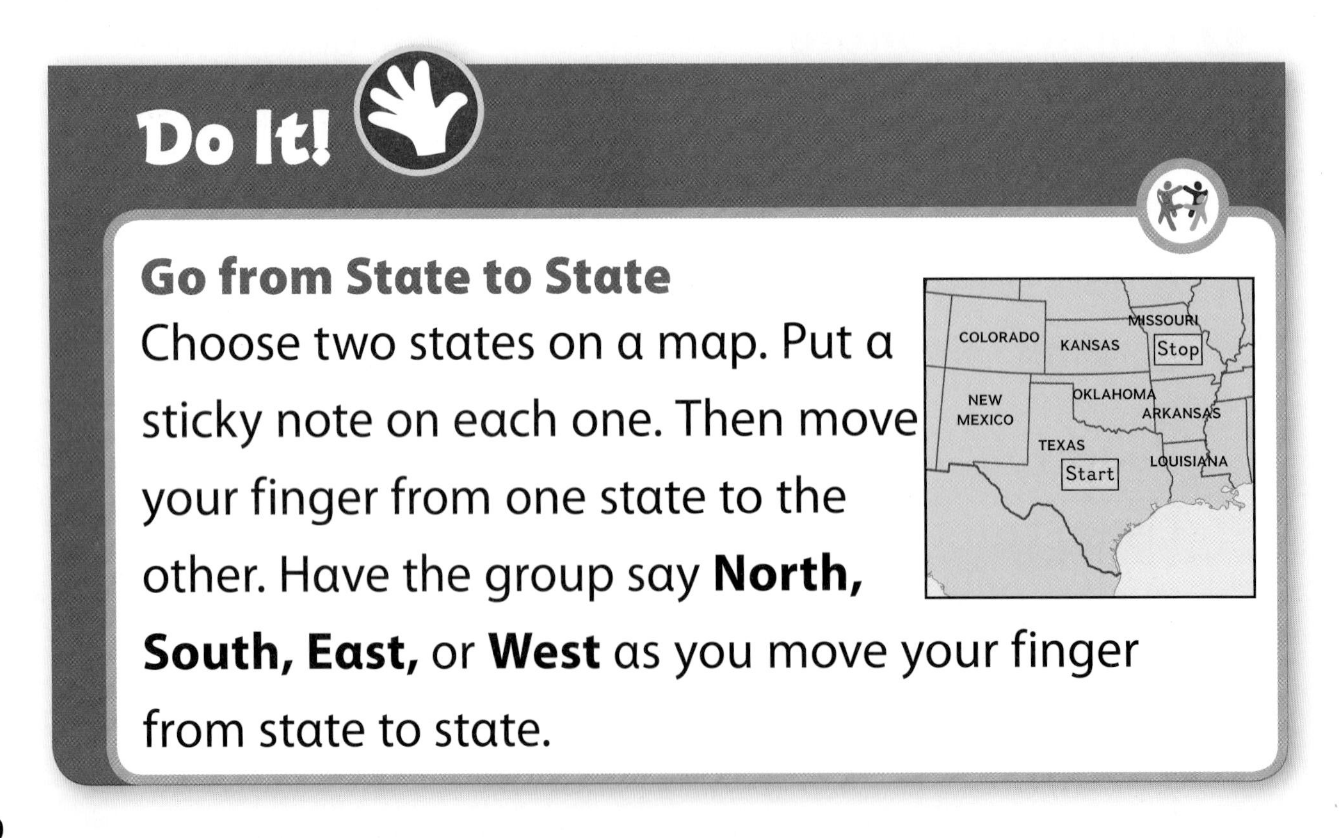

Do It!

Go from State to State

Choose two states on a map. Put a sticky note on each one. Then move your finger from one state to the other. Have the group say **North, South, East,** or **West** as you move your finger from state to state.

Talk About It!

Give Directions

Hide an object, such as a crayon. Then give good directions so that your partner can find the object. Take turns.

Go to the plants near the window. Look between the books.

Write It!

Draw a Map

Draw a map of your neighborhood. Use symbols in your map. Draw a map key that shows what the symbols stand for.

a b c d e f g h i j k l m n o p q r s t u v w x y z

A

alike

*These cats look **alike**.*

B

back

*The **back** tire is flat.*

beak

*This bird's **beak** is colorful.*

better

*Martha got a **better** grade.*

between

*The house is **between** the two trees.*

blow

*The wind will **blow** the tree down.*

body

*A baby has a small **body**.*

build

*You can **build** things with blocks.*

C

calendar

*This **calendar** shows the month of December.*

climb

*Orangutans can **climb** trees.*

cloudy

*It is a **cloudy** day.*

cold

*The snow is **cold**.*

communicate

People ***communicate*** *by talking and writing.*

computer

Jim does work on a ***computer****.*

cool

The fan keeps me ***cool****.*

corner

I write my name in the ***corner*** *of the paper.*

coverings

Birds and turtles have different ***coverings****.*

D

different

*These fruits are **different**.*

direction

*North is a **direction**.*

distance

*This man runs a long **distance**.*

E

easier

*It is **easier** to carry the books one at a time.*

east (East)

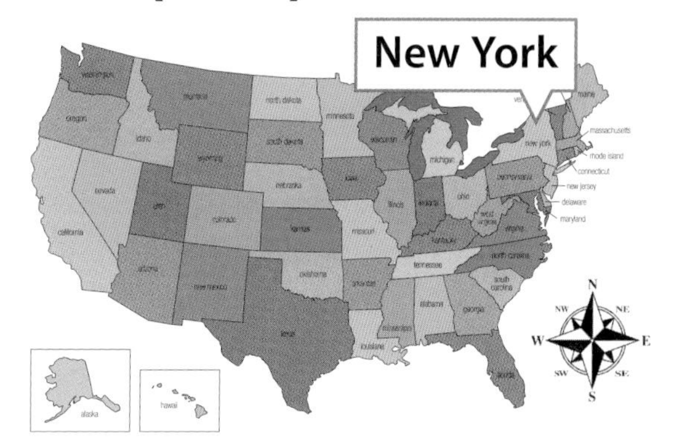

*New York is on the **east** coast of the United States.*

F

fact

*It's a **fact** that a dog has four legs.*

far

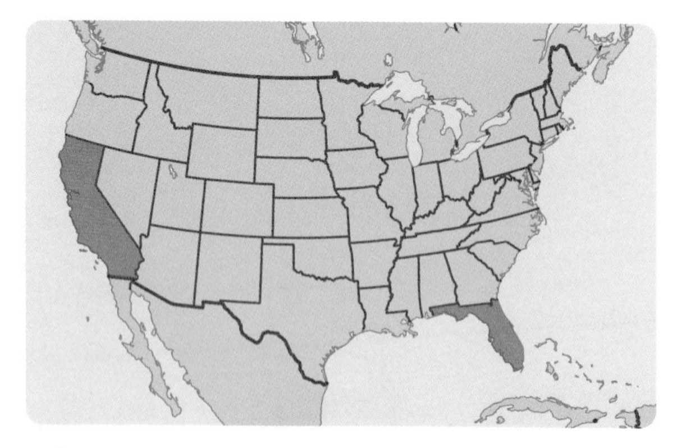

*The orange states are **far** from each other.*

fast

*This car is going **fast**.*

feathers

*This eagle's **feathers** help it to fly.*

feature

*A long neck is the main **feature** of a giraffe.*

feel

*The rabbit's fur **feels** soft.*

fly

*The gulls **fly** together.*

follow

Follow *the path through the grass.*

front

The ***front*** *of the house is blue.*

fur

This big dog has a lot of ***fur****.*

future

past — present — future

kindergarden — first grade — second grade

In the ***future*** *I will be in second grade.*

H

history

Study ***history*** *to learn what happened long ago.*

hot

Do not touch! The stove is ***hot****.*

I

Internet

*Sarah reads good news on the **Internet**.*

invent

*People **invent** things like the telephone.*

K

key

*A map **key** uses symbols to show where things are.*

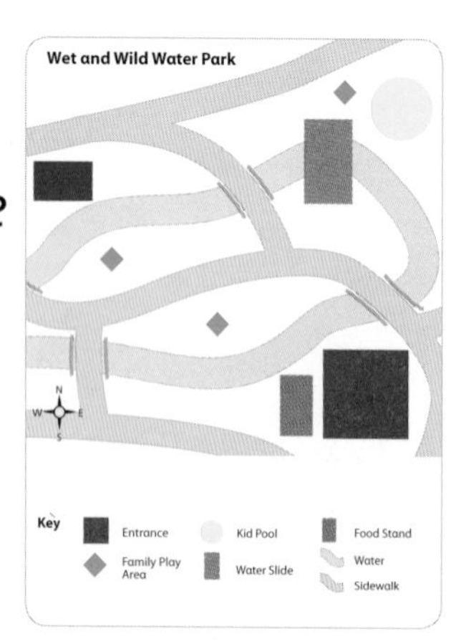

L

left

*Turn **left** when you see this sign.*

location

*Our tent is in a good **location** by the lake.*

look

*These apples **look** the same.*

M

machine

*This **machine** washes dishes.*

map

*This **map** shows where they are.*

meaning

*The dictionary shows us the **meaning** of words.*

message

*Jane got a text **message**.*

modern

*The cell phone is more **modern** than the old phone.*

month

*Our favorite **month** is July.*

a b c d e f g h i j k l m n o p q r s t u v w x y z

N

mouth

*This crocodile has a large **mouth**.*

movement

*The **movement** of a tortoise is slow.*

music

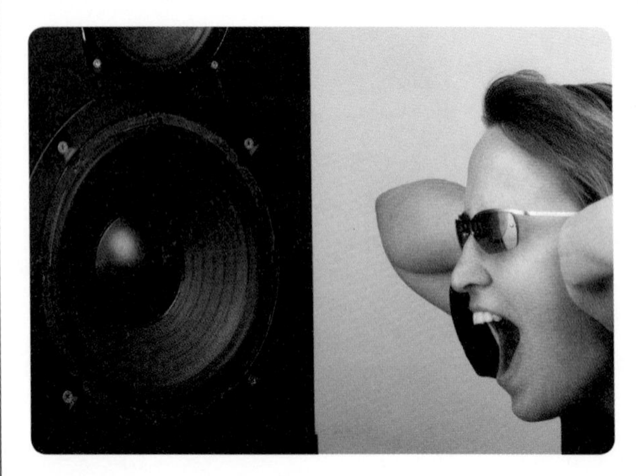

*This **music** is very loud.*

near

*I sit **near** the window.*

new

*This family has a **new** baby.*

news

*He is watching the **news** on TV.*

north (North)

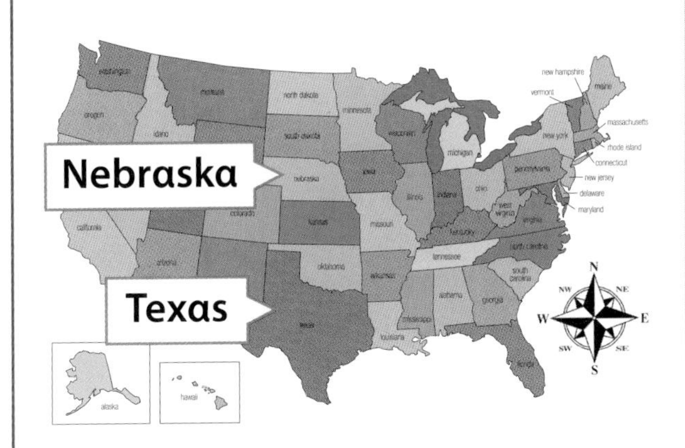

Nebraska is ***north*** *of Texas.*

now

The test starts right ***now****.*

O

old

This car is very ***old****.*

outside

They play ***outside****.*

P

parts

This engine has many ***parts****.*

past

past	**present**	**future**
kindergarden	first grade	second grade

In the ***past*** *I was in kindergarten.*

a b c d e f g h i j k l m n o p q r s t u v w x y z

path

*This **path** goes through the woods.*

paw

*This is a cat's **paw**.*

picture

*These **pictures** sit on a desk.*

power

*This toaster uses **power**.*

present

past	present	future
kindergarden	first grade	second grade

*Today is the **present**. I am in first grade.*

push

*We had to **push** the car.*

R

rainy

*It is a **rainy** day.*

record

*This old **record** has some fun music.*

right

*Turn **right** when you see this sign.*

run

*We like to **run** during recess.*

S

scales

*The **scales** on this snake are beautiful.*

show

*I **show** my drawing.*

sign

*This **sign** means to add.*

slide

*We like to **slide** at the park.*

slither

*The snake **slithers** across the ground.*

snowy

*This mountain is very **snowy**.*

soft

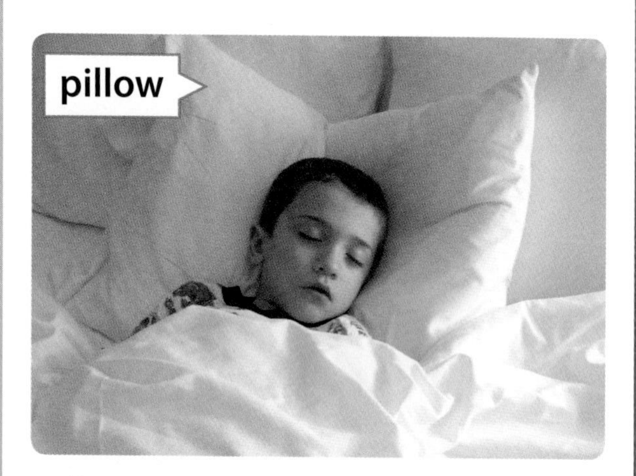

*Pillows are **soft**.*

south (South)

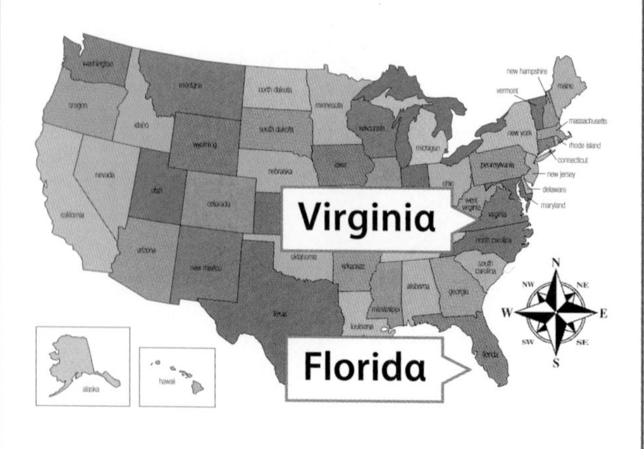

*Florida is **south** of Virginia.*

storm

*Our family stays inside when there is a **storm**.*

strong

*We are **strong**.*

sunny

*It is a **sunny** day.*

swim

*We like to **swim** in the pool.*

symbol

*This flag is a **symbol** of America.*

T

tail

*This lemur has a long **tail**.*

temperature

*It's cold! The **temperature** is only 8° Fahrenheit.*

then

*Back **then**, I didn't know how to walk.*

tool

*A dictionary is a **tool** you can use to look up words.*

U

useful

*This hammer is very **useful**.*

W

warm

*The blanket keeps us **warm**.*

weather

*We like the warm **weather**.*

west (West)

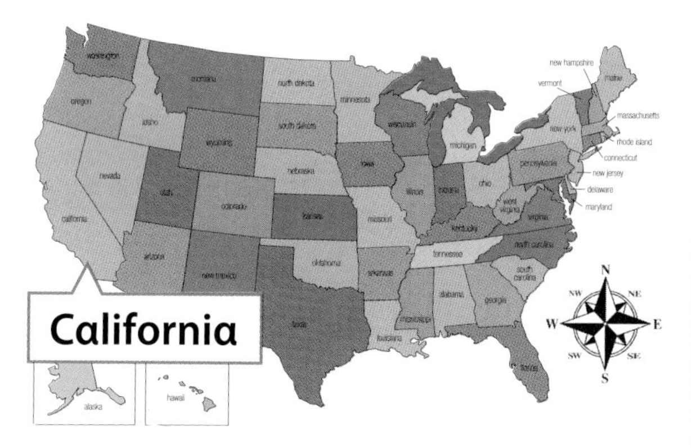

California is on the ***west*** *coast of the United States.*

wind

The ***wind*** *is very strong today.*

Y

year

This has been a fun ***year****.*

Index

D

E

F

G

Authors

Illustrators

Acknowledgments, continued

Text Credits

Unit Five

Unit Six

Unit Seven

Unit Eight

NATIONAL GEOGRAPHIC SCHOOL PUBLISHING

National Geographic School Publishing gratefully acknowledges the contributions of the following National Geographic Explorers to our program and to our planet:

Josh Thorne, 2008 National Geographic Emerging Explorer
Michael Fay, National Geographic Explorer-in-Residence
Cid Simoes and Paola Segura, 2008 National Geographic Emerging Explorers
Mariana Fuentes, National Geographic Grantee
Greg Marshall, National Geographic Scientist
Tim Samaras, 2005 National Geographic Emerging Explorer
Constance Adams, 2005 National Geographic Emerging Explorer
Michael DiSpezio, National Geographic Presenter

Photographic Credits

iv (tl) Kevin Schafer/Alamy Images. v (tc) Carsten Peter/National Geographic Image Collection. vi (tl) Museum of the City of New York/Corbis. vii (tc) Corbis Premium RF/Alamy Images. ix (tr) Corbis Premium RF/Alamy Images. 2-3 (bg) Arco Images GmbH/Alamy Images. 3 (inset) Liz Garza Williams/Hampton-Brown/National Geographic School Publishing. 5 (bl) PhotoDisc/Getty Images. (br) PhotoDisc/Getty Images. (cl) Eric Isselée/iStockphoto. (cr) Eric Isselée/Shutterstock. (tl) NatUlrich/Shutterstock. (tr) Michael Lynch/Alamy Images. 6 (bl) DigitalStock/Corbis. (br) Brand X Pictures/Jupiterimages. (tl) Jello5700/iStockphoto. (tr) Edwin Verin/Shutterstock. 7 (bc) Artville. (bl) Michele Burgess/Corbis. (br) Artville. (tcl) Rosemarie Gearhart/iStockphoto. (tcr) Artville. (tl) Alan Carey/Corbis. (tr) PhotoDisc/Getty Images. 30 MBI/Alamy Images. 31 teve Snowden/iStockphoto. 33 Heidi and Hans-Jurgen Koch/Minden Pictures/National Geographic Image Collection. 34 Otis Imboden/National Geographic Image Collection. 35 Kevin Schafer/Alamy Images. 36-37 John Zellmer/iStockphoto. 38 Kevin Schafer/Alamy Images. 39 PhotoDisc/Getty Images. 40 Ljupco/iStockphoto. 41 (bl) Corbis/Jupiterimages. (br) Frans Lemmens/Corbis. (cl) Dan Guravich/Corbis. (cr) Luiz Claudio Marigo/Nature Picture Library. (tl) John Foxx Images/Imagestate. (tr) Creatas/Jupiterimages. 42 (l) Abramova Kseniya/Shutterstock. (r) Andreas Weiss/Shutterstock. 43 (bl) age fotostock/SuperStock. (br) PE Forsberg/Alamy Images. (tc) Anna Sedneva/Shutterstock. (tl) Nick Kirk/Alamy Images. (tr) colin streater/Alamy Images. 44 (inset) Frank Leung/iStockphoto. 44-45 (bg) Rich Lindie/Shutterstock. 46 (b) Paul Tessier/iStockphoto. (t) Frank Leung/iStockphoto. 47 (b) Paul Chesley/Getty Images. (t) Fivespots/Shutterstock. 48 (b) John Carnemolla/Shutterstock. (t) Eric Isselée/iStockphoto. 49 Alexia Khruscheva/Shutterstock. 50 (b) Matt Abbe/iStockphoto. (t) pkruger/iStockphoto. 51 EcoPrint/Shutterstock. 52 Eric Isselée/iStockphoto. 53 Wojciech Jaskowski/Shutterstock. 54 H Lansdown/Alamy Images. 55 Edd Westmacott/Alamy Images. 56 (b) Ron Heijman/iStockphoto. (t) Eric Isselée/iStockphoto. 57 (b) Ingram Publishing/Superstock. (t) Wayne Tam/iStockphoto. 59 Michael DeLeon/iStockphoto. 60 (l) Eric Isselée/Shutterstock. (r) pkruger/iStockphoto. 61 (bg) Hampton-Brown/National Geographic School Publishing. (l) National Geographic Image Collection. (r) EuToch/iStockphoto. 62 (b) Dr. Michael Heithaus. (t) Mark Mallchok/Brella Productions. 62-63 (bg) Hampton-Brown/National Geographic School Publishing. 63 (b) Greg Marshall/National Geographic Image Collection. (t) National Geographic Image Collection. 64 (bl) Matt Abbe/iStockphoto. (br) Dr. Michael Heithaus. (rbg) Hampton-Brown/National Geographic School Publishing. (tl) pkruger/iStockphoto. (tr) Mark Mallchok/Brella Productions. 65 (bl) Stefan Klein/iStockphoto. (br) Stefan Klein/iStockphoto. 66 John Zellmer/iStockphoto. 68 Arco Images GmbH/Alamy Images. 69 (l) Blend Images/SuperStock. (r) Blend Images/SuperStock. 70-71 (bg) Warren Faidley/Corbis. 71 (inset) Liz Garza Williams/Hampton-Brown/National Geographic School Publishing. 73 (bl) Michael Rolands/iStockphoto. (br) ND1939/iStockphoto. (tl) Zastol`skiy Victor Leonidovich/Shutterstock. (tr) cristovao/Shutterstock. 74 Corbis/Jupiterimages. 75 (bl) Nicholas Eveleigh/Alamy Images. (br) Jim Arbogast/Digital Vision/Jupiterimages. (tc) Polka Dot Images/Jupiterimages. (tl) David Madison/Digital Vision/Jupiterimages. (tr) Design Pics/Jupiterimages. 95 (l) Nicole S. Young/iStockphoto. (r) Sean Locke/iStockphoto. 105 (bl) Antonio Jorge Nunes/Shutterstock. (br) sebos/Shutterstock. (cr) Sam Abell/National Geographic Image Collection. (tl) Image Source. (tr) Randy Faris/Corbis. 106 Digital Vision/Getty Images. 107 (bl) Skip O'Donnell/iStockphoto. (tc) Nick Kennedy/Alamy Images. (tl) George F. Mobley/National Geographic Image Collection. (tr) David Chasey/Photodisc/Jupiterimages. (tr) David Hardman/iStockphoto. 125 Michael Wolff. 127 Blend Images/Alamy Images. 129 Carsten Peter/National Geographic Image Collection. 130 (b) Warren Faidley/Corbis. (c) Mark Thiessen/National Geographic Image Collection. (t) Hampton-Brown/National Geographic School Publishing. 130-131 (bg) Carsten Peter/National Geographic Image Collection. 132 Carsten Peter/National Geographic Image Collection. 133 (b) PhotoDisc/Getty Images. (t) Mark Thiessen/National Geographic Image Collection. 136 Warren Faidley/Corbis. 137 (b) Rick Holcomb/Hampton-Brown/National Geographic School Publishing. (t) Jose Luis Pelaez Inc/Blend Images/Jupiterimages. 138 (inset) Brasil2/iStockphoto. 138-139 (bg) Jupiterimages/Getty Images. 139 (inset) Getty Images/Jupiterimages. 141 (bl) George Marks/Getty Images. (br) Image Source/Alamy Images. (cl) George Marks/Getty Images. (cr) Pali Rao/iStockphoto. (tl) George Marks/Getty Images. (tr) Nina Shannon/iStockphoto. 142 MIXA/Alamy Images. 143 (l) PhotoAlto/Alamy Images. (r) Bettmann/Corbis. 144 (bl) North Wind Picture Archives. (br) SSPL/The Image Works, Inc. (tc) Oxford Science Archive / Heritage-Images/The Image Works, Inc. (tl) SSPL/The Image Works, Inc. (tr) SSPL/The Image Works, Inc. 145 (b) Fancy/Alamy Images. (t) Minnesota Historical Society/Corbis. 146-147 CRG Studios/Blend Images/Jupiterimages. 148 Pierre Vauthey/Corbis Sygma. 149 Michael Newman/PhotoEdit. 150 (b) Emilia Stasiak/Shutterstock. (t) The Granger Collection, New York. 151 (b) Photosani/Shutterstock. (t) Lester Lefkowitz/Taxi/Getty Images. 152 (b) Adrio Communications Ltd/Shutterstock. (t) Bettmann/Corbis. 153 (bg) BananaStock/Jupiterimages. (inset) Bettmann/Corbis. 154 (b) cyphix-photo/Shutterstock. (t) SuperStock. 155 (b) Elly Godfroy/Alamy Images. (t) Image Source/Corbis. 156 (bg) Museum of the City of New York/Corbis. (inset) Old Paper Studios/Alamy Images. 157 (b) Sean Locke/iStockphoto. (t) David Young-Wolff/PhotoEdit. 158 FPG/Getty Images. 159 Corbis Premium RF/Alamy Images. 160 (bl) North Wind Picture Archives. (br) SSPL/The Image Works, Inc. (tl) SSPL/The Image Works, Inc. (tr) Oxford Science Archive / Heritage-Images/The Image Works, Inc. 161 (bl) Topham/The Image Works, Inc. (br) michael ledray/Shutterstock. (tl) SSPL/The Image Works, Inc. (tr) SSPL/The Image Works, Inc. 162 (l) Liz Garza Williams/Hampton-Brown/National Geographic School Publishing. (r) PhotoDisc/Getty Images. 163 (l) Donna Coleman/iStockphoto. (r) Sean Locke/iStockphoto. 164 (l) Rob Marmion/Shutterstock. (r) Christophe Testi/Alamy Images. 165 (bg) PhotoDisc/Getty Images. (c) Mark Thiessen/Hampton-Brown/National Geographic School Publishing. (inset) NASA Human Space Flight Gallery. 166 (inset) NASA - GRIN (Great Images in NASA). 166-167 (bg) PhotoDisc/Getty Images. 167 (b) PhotoDisc/Getty Images. (t) NASA Human Space Flight Gallery. 168 (inset) NASA Human Space Flight Gallery. 168-169 (bg) PhotoDisc/Getty Images. 169 (inset) NASA Human Space Flight Gallery. 174 Liz Garza Williams/Hampton-Brown/National Geographic School Publishing. 175 (bc) Image Club. (bl) Sergey Peterman/Shutterstock. (br) Sebastian Crocker/Shutterstock. (tc) Holly Kuchera/Shutterstock. (tl) Asia Images Group Pte Ltd/Alamy Images. (tr) Irina Fischer/Shutterstock. 189 Chuku Lee/Pat Cummings. 190 (bc) Sibrikov Valery/Shutterstock. (bl) ajt/Shutterstock. (c) Elena Elisseeva/Shutterstock. (t) Kamyshko/Shutterstock. 192 (l) JGI/Jamie Grill/Jupiterimages. (r) Bozena/Shutterstock. 200 FPG/Getty Images. 201 Liz Garza Williams/Hampton-Brown/National

Geographic School Publishing. 202 (bg) Jupiterimages/Getty Images. (inset) Brasil2/iStockphoto. 203 (b) Yulli/Shutterstock. (t) Liz Garza Williams/Hampton-Brown/National Geographic School Publishing. 204 (inset) Liz Garza Williams/Hampton-Brown/National Geographic School Publishing. 204-205 (bg) Alaska Stock Images/age fotostock. 207 (cr) Michael Mattner/iStockphoto. 209 (bl) GlowImages/Alamy Images. (tl) Domenico Pellegriti/iStockphoto. (tr) PhotoDisc/Getty Images. 210-211 (bg) Sharon Day/Shutterstock. 211 (inset) Corbis Premium RF/Alamy Images. 212 eldirector77/Shutterstock. 213 Sharon Day/Shutterstock. 214 Steve Geer/iStockphoto. 215 Sharon Day/Shutterstock. 216 Chad McDermott/Shutterstock. 217 (bg) Sharon Day/Shutterstock. (inset) Fotocrisis/Shutterstock. 218 mihalec/Shutterstock. 219 Sharon Day/Shutterstock. 220 Sonja Fagnan/iStockphoto. 221 Sharon Day/Shutterstock. 222-223 (bg) Sharon Day/Shutterstock. (inset) STILLFX/Shutterstock. 225 indeed/Jupiterimages. 226 (l) Stacey Lynn Payne/Shutterstock. (r) Stacey Lynn Payne/Shutterstock. 235 (bl) Ben Blankenburg/iStockphoto. (br) Corbis. (tl) Tischenko Irina/Shutterstock. (tr) Diane N. Ennis/Shutterstock. 257 Claire Deroche/Argentina Palacios. 259 Liz Garza Williams/Hampton-Brown/National Geographic School Publishing. 261 (bg) Clearviewstock/Alamy Images. (inset) Eyecandy Images/Alamy Images. 262 (bcl, bl, c, tlc) Mark Thiessen/Hampton-Brown/National Geographic School Publishing. (tl) rusm/iStockphoto. (tr) Morgan Lane Photography/Shutterstock. 262-263 (bg) Clearviewstock/Alamy Images. 263 (b, t) Mark Thiessen/Hampton-Brown/National Geographic School Publishing. 264 (b, t) Mark Thiessen/Hampton-Brown/National Geographic School Publishing. 264-265 (bg) Clearviewstock/Alamy Images. 265 (b,t) Mark Thiessen/Hampton-Brown/National Geographic School Publishing. 266 (b, t) Mark Thiessen/Hampton-Brown/National Geographic School Publishing. (bg) Clearviewstock/Alamy Images. (t) Mark Thiessen/Hampton-Brown/National Geographic School Publishing. 267 Mark Thiessen/Hampton-Brown/National Geographic School Publishing. 270 Alaska Stock Images/age fotostock. 271 kate_sept2004/iStockphoto. 296 (bl) John Foxx Images/Imagestate. (br) photobank.kiev.ua/Shutterstock. (cl) Nick Kirk/Alamy Images. (cr) Domenico Pellegriti/iStockphoto. (tl) Alan Carey/Corbis. (tr) Jon Feingersh/Getty Images. 297 (bl) Alex Slobodkin/iStockphoto. (br) George F. Mobley/National Geographic Image Collection. (cl) Asia Images Group Pte Ltd/Alamy Images. (tl) Rosemarie Gearhart/iStockphoto. (tr) Csaba Vanyi/Shutterstock. 298 (bl) Nick Kennedy/Alamy Images. (br) Ryan M. Bolton/Shutterstock. (cl) Image Source Pink/Alamy Images. (cr) Creatas/Jupiterimages. (tl) PhotoAlto/Alamy Images. 299 (bl) PhotoDisc/Getty Images. (br) Anna Sedneva/Shutterstock. (cl) Tischenko Irina/Shutterstock. (cr) jamie cross/Shutterstock. (tc) PhotoDisc/Getty Images. (tl) Artville. (tr) Blend Images/Alamy Images. 300 (bl) PureStock/SuperStock. (bl) Michael and Patricia Fogden/Minden Pictures/National Geographic Image Collection. (br) PhotoDisc/Getty Images. (cl) David Madison/Digital Vision/Jupiterimages. (cr) cynoclub/Shutterstock. (tr) Polka Dot Images/Jupiterimages. 301 (bl) Corel. (br) David Chasey/Photodisc/Jupiterimages. (cl) colin streater/Alamy Images. (cr) Bettmann/Corbis. (tl) Diane N. Ennis/Shutterstock. 302 (cl) Holly Kuchera/Shutterstock. (cr) Ben Blankenburg/iStockphoto. (tl) Image Source/Alamy Images. (tr) Clint Scholz/iStockphoto. 303 (bl) Thomas M Perkins/Shutterstock. (bl) Image Source/Alamy Images. (cc) Sergey Peterman/Shutterstock. (cl) Creatas Images/Jupiterimages. (cr) Image Club. (tl) Irina Fischer/Shutterstock. (tr) BananaStock/Jupiterimages. 304 (bl) Zsolt, Biczó/Shutterstock. (br) Ulrich Niehoff/imagebroker/Alamy Images. (cl) age fotostock/SuperStock. (cr) Thomas Perkins/iStockphoto. (tl) Robert Madden/National Geographic Image Collection. (tl) Corbis. 305 (bl) Howard Noel/iStockphoto. (cl) Michael Newman/PhotoEdit. (cr) Artville. (tc) erdem/Shutterstock. (tl) jamie cross/Shutterstock. (tr) Polka Dot Images/Jupiterimages. 306 (bl) Image Source/Jupiterimages. (br) PE Forsberg/Alamy Images. (cl) Wolf Design/Shutterstock. (tl) John Foxx Images/Imagestate. (tr) Design Pics/Jupiterimages. 307 (bl) Amanda Rohde/iStockphoto. (br) GlowImages/Alamy Images. (cl) Sven Hoppe/Shutterstock. (cr) DigitalStock/Corbis. (tl) Melville B. Grosvenor/National Geographic Image Collection. (tr) Jose Luis Pelaez Inc/Jupiterimages. 308 (bc) jamie cross/Shutterstock. (bl) Heinrich van den Berg/Getty Images. (br) erdem/Shutterstock. (cl) Digital Vision/Getty Images. (cr) Nicholas Eveleigh/Alamy Images. (tr) Photodisc/Getty Images. 309 (bl) Eric Gevaert/iStockphoto. (br) Martin Harvey/Alamy Images. (cl) Jim Arbogast/Digital Vision/Jupiterimages. (cr) Lee Prince/Shutterstock. (tl) Petar Paunchev/Alamy Images. (tr) John Giustina/Getty Images. 310 (bl) Sebastian Crocker/Shutterstock. (br) P. Broze & A. Chederros/ONOKY - Photononstop/Alamy Images. (cl) Image Box Uk Ltd/Alamy Images. (cr) Skip O'Donnell/iStockphoto. (tl) David Hardman/iStockphoto. (tr) Blend Images/Jose Luis Pelaez Inc/Getty Images. 311 (bl) James Osmond/Alamy Images. (cl) Mike Theiss/National Geographic Image Collection. (tl) jamie cross/Shutterstock. (tr) erdem/Shutterstock.

Illustrator Credits

4 Peter Grosshauser. 34 Mapping Specialists, Ltd. 72 Alessia Girasole. 97–101 Amanda Hall. 104 Don Tate. 128 Alessia Girasole. 140 Rob McClurkan; 172-173 Red Hansen; 176-189 Frank Morrison; 196 Sachiko Yoshikawa; 198 Frank Morrison. 206–208, 210 Rob McClurkan. 213, 215, 217, 219, 221 Annie Bissett. 224 Rob McClurkan. 227–231 Anne Wilson. 232 Steve Bjorkman. 233 Jannie Ho. 234 Steve Bjorkman. 235 Mapping Specialists, Ltd. 236–258, 260, 266, 268 Valeria Docampo. 270 Mapping Specialists, Ltd.

English Language Proficiency Standards (ELPS)
English Language Arts and Reading (ELAR) TEKS

UNIT 5 Creature Features		
2–3	Unit Opener **Share What You Know** **Build Background Video**	**ELPS** • **1.A.** use prior knowledge and experiences to understand meanings in English • **4.F.5** use visual and contextual support to develop background knowledge needed to comprehend increasingly challenging language **ELAR TEKS** • **G1.16.A.1** recognize different purposes of media (with adult assistance) • **G1.27.B.1** follow instructions that involve a short related sequence of actions
4	Language **Compare and Contrast**	**ELPS** • **1.F.** use accessible language and learn new and essential language in the process • **2.E.3** use linguistic support to enhance and confirm understanding of increasingly complex and elaborated spoken language • **2.F.2** listen to and derive meaning from a variety of media to build and reinforce language attainment • **3.B.1** expand and internalize initial English vocabulary by learning and using high-frequency English words necessary for identifying and describing people, places, and objects • **3.B.3** expand and internalize initial English vocabulary by learning and using routine language needed for classroom communication • **4.F.4** use visual and contextual support to develop grasp of language structures needed to comprehend increasingly challenging language
5, 7	Science Vocabulary Academic Vocabulary **Key Words** **Talk Together**	**ELPS** • **3.D.** speak using content area vocabulary in context to internalize new English words and build academic language proficiency • **4.F.3** use visual and contextual support to develop vocabulary needed to comprehend increasingly challenging language • **4.F 8, 9, 10** use support from peers and teachers to develop vocabulary, grasp of language structures, and background knowledge needed to comprehend increasingly challenging language **ELAR TEKS** • **G1.6.C.1** determine what words mean from how they are used in a sentence, either heard or read • **G1.28.A.2** share ideas about the topic under discussion, speaking clearly at an appropriate pace, using the conventions of language
6	Thinking Map **Compare and Contrast** **Talk Together**	**ELPS** • **2.E.1, 2** use visual and contextual support support to enhance and confirm understanding of increasingly complex and elaborated spoken language • **2.G.3, 6, 9** understand the general meaning, main points, and details of spoken language ranging from situations in which contexts are familiar to unfamiliar • **4.D.1** use prereading supports to enhance comprehension of written text
For Pete's Sake		
8–29	**Genre:** Animal Fantasy **Characters** **Reading Strategy: Make Connections**	**ELPS** • **4.F.6** use support from peers and teachers to read grade-level appropriate content area text • **4.G.1** demonstrate comprehension of increasingly complex English by participating in shared reading • **4.I.1** demonstrate English comprehension by employing basic reading skills • **4.J** demonstrate English comprehension and expand reading skills by employing inferential skills and finding supporting text evidence **ELAR TEKS** • **G1.RC-1.F.1** make connections to own experiences
30	Think and Respond **Talk About It** **Write About It**	**ELPS** • **1.E.3** internalize new academic language by using and reusing it in meaningful ways in speaking activities that build concept and language attainment • **1.E.4** internalize new academic language by using and reusing it in meaningful ways in writing activities that build concept and language attainment • **1.H** develop and expand repertoire of learning strategies • **2.H.1** understand implicit ideas in increasingly complex spoken language commensurate with grade-level learning expectations • **3.D.2** speak using content area vocabulary in context to build academic language proficiency • **4.1.2** expand reading skills • **4.F.7** use support from peers and teachers to enhance and confirm understanding • **4.G.3** demonstrate comprehension of increasingly complex English by responding to questions • **4.K** demonstrate English comprehension and expand reading skills by employing analytical skills such as evaluating written information and performing critical analysis • **5.B.2** write using content-based grade-level vocabulary **ELAR TEKS** • **G1.4.B.4** locate details about stories • **G1.RC-1.F.1** make connections to own experiences

UNIT 5 Creature Features, *continued*		
31	Reread and Compare **Compare Characters**	**ELPS** • **4.K** demonstrate English comprehension and expand reading skills by employing analytical skills • **3.H.2** describe with increasing specificity and detail as more English is acquired • **4.I.2** expand reading skills **ELAR TEKS** • **G1.9.B.1** describe characters in a story
32	Word Work **Synonyms**	**ELPS** • **4.F.3** use visual and contextual support to develop vocabulary needed to comprehend increasingly challenging language
38	Respond and Extend **Compare Genres** **Talk Together**	**ELPS** • **2.G.1** understand the general meaning of spoken language ranging from situations in which topics are familiar to unfamiliar • **4.K** demonstrate English comprehension and expand reading skills by employing analytical skills such as evaluating written information and performing critical analysis
39	Grammar **Complete Sentences**	**ELPS** • **3.C.2** speak using a variety of sentence lengths with increasing accuracy and ease • **3.C.3** speak using a variety of sentence types with increasing accuracy and ease • **4.F.4** use visual and contextual support to develop grasp of language structures needed to comprehend increasingly challenging language **ELAR TEKS** • **G1.20.B.1** speak in complete sentences with correct subject-verb agreement • **G1.21.B.1.i** recognize basic capitalization for the beginning of sentences • **G1.21.B.2.i** use basic capitalization for the beginning of sentences • **G1.21.C.1** recognize punctuation marks at the end of declarative sentences • **G1.21.C.4** use punctuation marks at the end of declarative sentences
40	Language **Give Information**	**ELPS** • **1.F.** use accessible language and learn new and essential language in the process • **2.E.3** use linguistic support to enhance and confirm understanding of increasingly complex and elaborated spoken language • **2.F.2** listen to and derive meaning from a variety of media to build and reinforce language attainment • **2.H.2** understand information in increasingly complex spoken language commensurate with grade-level learning expectations • **3.F.2** give information ranging from concrete vocabulary to abstract and content-based vocabulary • **4.F.4** use visual and contextual support to develop grasp of language structures needed to comprehend increasingly challenging language
41, 43	Science Vocabulary Academic Vocabulary **Key Words** **Talk Together**	**ELPS** • **2.G.1** understand the general meaning of spoken language ranging from situations in which topics are familiar to unfamiliar • **3.D.1** speak using content area vocabulary in context to internalize new English words • **4.F 3, 8, 9, 10** use visual and contextual support, support from peers and teachers to develop vocabulary, grasp of language structures, and background knowledge needed to comprehend increasingly challenging language **ELAR TEKS** • **G1.6.C.1** determine what words mean from how they are used in a sentence, either heard or read • **G1.28.A.2** share ideas about the topic under discussion, speaking clearly at an appropriate pace, using the conventions of language
42	Thinking Map **Categorize Details** **Talk Together**	**ELPS** • **2.E.1, 2** use visual and contextual support support to enhance and confirm understanding of increasingly complex and elaborated spoken language • **2.G.4, 7** understand the main points and details of spoken language ranging from situations in which topics are familiar to unfamiliar • **4.D.1** use prereading supports to enhance comprehension of written text
Slither, Slide, Hop, and Run		
44–57	**Genre:** Fact Book **Reading Strategy: Make Connections**	**ELPS** • **4.F.6** use support from peers and teachers to read grade-level appropriate content area text • **4.G.1** demonstrate comprehension of increasingly complex English by participating in shared reading • **4.I.1** demonstrate English comprehension by employing basic reading skills • **4.J** demonstrate English comprehension and expand reading skills by employing inferential skills and finding supporting text evidence **ELAR TEKS** • **G1.RC-1.F.2** make connections to ideas in other texts • **G1.RC-1.F.3** make connections to the larger community

58	Think and Respond **Talk About It** **Write About It**	**ELPS** • **1.E.3, 4** internalize new academic language by using and reusing it in meaningful ways in speaking and writing activities that build concept and language attainment • **1.H** develop and expand repertoire of learning strategies • **3.D.2** speak using content area vocabulary in context to build academic language proficiency • **4.F.7** use support from peers and teachers to enhance and confirm understanding • **4.G.3** demonstrate comprehension of increasingly complex English by responding to questions • **4.K** demonstrate English comprehension and expand reading skills by employing analytical skills • **4.I.2** expand reading skills • **5.B.2** write using content-based grade-level vocabulary **ELAR TEKS** • **G1.4.B.7** locate facts about other texts • **G1.4.B.8** locate details about other texts • **G1.14.B** identify important facts and details in text, heard or read • **G1.RC-1.F.2** make connections to ideas in other texts
59	Reread and Summarize **Categorize Details**	**ELPS** • **4.G.2** demonstrate comprehension of increasingly complex English by retelling or summarizing material • **4.I.2** expand reading skills
60	Word Work **Antonyms**	**ELPS** • **4.F.3** use visual and contextual support to develop vocabulary needed to comprehend increasingly challenging language
64	Respond and Extend **Compare Genres** **Talk Together**	**ELPS** • **2.G.1** understand the general meaning of spoken language ranging from situations in which topics are familiar to unfamiliar • **4.F.8** use support from peers and teachers to develop vocabulary needed to comprehend increasingly challenging language • **4.K** demonstrate English comprehension and expand reading skills by employing analytical skills
65	Grammar and Spelling **Subject-Verb Agreement**	**ELPS** • **3.C.2** speak using a variety of sentence lengths with increasing accuracy and ease • **3.C.3** speak using a variety of sentence types with increasing accuracy and ease • **4.F.4** use visual and contextual support to develop grasp of language structures needed to comprehend increasingly challenging language • **5.C.2, 3** employ English spelling patterns and rules with increasing accuracy **ELAR TEKS** • **G1.20.B.1** speak in complete sentences with correct subject-verb agreement
66–67	Writing Project **Write Like a Scientist (Write an Article)** **Plan and Write**	**ELPS** • **1.G.** demonstrate an increasing ability to distinguish between, and knowledge of when to use, formal and informal English **ELAR TEKS** • **G1.17.A.1** plan a first draft by generating ideas for writing • **G1.17.B.1** develop drafts by sequencing ideas through writing sentences • **G1.19.A.1** write brief compositions about topics of interest to the student
66–67	Writing Project continued **Write Like a Scientist (Write an Article)** **Check Your Work**	**ELPS** • **5.C.1, 2** spell familiar English words and employ English spelling rules with increasing accuracy • **5.F.1** write using a variety of grade-level appropriate sentence lengths in increasingly accurate way **ELAR TEKS** • **G1.17.C.** revise drafts by adding or deleting a word, phrase, or sentence • **G1.17.D.** edit drafts for grammar, punctuation, and spelling using a teacher-developed rubric
66–67	Writing Project continued **Write Like a Scientist (Write an Article)** **Finish and Share**	**ELPS** • **3.E.1** share information in cooperative learning interactions • **3.I.** adapt spoken language appropriately for formal and informal purposes **ELAR TEKS** • **G1.17.E** publish and share writing with others
68–69	Share Your Ideas	**ELPS** • **2.I.** 4 demonstrate listening comprehension of increasingly complex spoken English by collaborating with peers commensurate with content and grade-level needs • **3.E.1** share information in cooperative learning interactions • **3.F.1** ask [for] information ranging from concrete vocabulary to abstract and content-based vocabulary • **3.I** adapt spoken language appropriately for formal and informal purposes **ELAR TEKS** • **G1.28.A.1** share information about the topic under discussion, speaking clearly at an appropriate pace, using the conventions of language • **G1.28.A.2** share ideas about the topic under discussion, speaking clearly at an appropriate pace, using the conventions of language

English Language Proficiency Standards (ELPS) English Language Arts and Reading (ELAR) TEKS, *continued*

UNIT 6 Up in the Air		
70–71	Unit Opener **Share What You Know** **Build Background Video**	**ELPS** • **1.A.** use prior knowledge and experiences to understand meanings in English • **4.F.5** use visual and contextual support to develop background knowledge needed to comprehend increasingly challenging language **ELAR TEKS** • **G1.16.A.1** recognize different purposes of media (with adult assistance) • **G1.27.B.1** follow instructions that involve a short related sequence of actions • **G1.28.A.2** share ideas about the topic under discussion, speaking clearly at an appropriate pace, using the conventions of language
72	Language **Explain**	**ELPS** • **1.F.** use accessible language and learn new and essential language in the process • **2.E.3** use linguistic support to enhance and confirm understanding of increasingly complex and elaborated spoken language • **2.F.2** listen to and derive meaning from a variety of media to build and reinforce language attainment • **2.H.2** understand information in increasingly complex spoken language commensurate with grade-level learning expectations • **3.H.3** explain with increasing specificity and detail as more English is acquired • **4.F.4** use visual and contextual support to develop grasp of language structures needed to comprehend increasingly challenging language
73, 75	Science Vocabulary Academic Vocabulary **Key Words** **Talk Together**	**ELPS** • **3.D.** speak using content area vocabulary in context to internalize new English words and build academic language proficiency • **3.H.3** explain with increasing specificity and detail as more English is acquired • **4.F 3, 8, 9, 10** use visual and contextual support, support from peers and teachers to develop vocabulary, grasp of language structures, and background knowledge needed to comprehend increasingly challenging language **ELAR TEKS** • **G1.6.C.1** determine what words mean from how they are used in a sentence, either heard or read • **G1.28.A.2** share ideas about the topic under discussion, speaking clearly at an appropriate pace, using the conventions of language
74	Thinking Map **Find Cause and Effect** **Talk Together**	**ELPS** • **2.E.1, 2** use visual and contextual support support to enhance and confirm understanding of increasingly complex and elaborated spoken language • **2.G.6, 9** understand the main points and details of spoken language ranging from situations in which contexts are familiar to unfamiliar • **2.I.4** demonstrate listening comprehension of increasingly complex spoken English by collaborating with peers commensurate with content and grade-level needs • **3.H.3** explain with increasing specificity and detail as more English is acquired • **4.D.1** use prereading supports to enhance comprehension of written text
I Face the Wind		
76–93	**Genre:** Science Nonfiction **Illustration** **Reading Strategy: Make Inferences**	**ELPS** • **2.H.2** understand information in increasingly complex spoken language commensurate with grade-level learning expectations • **4.F.6** use support from peers and teachers to read grade-level appropriate content area text • **4.G.1** demonstrate comprehension of increasingly complex English by participating in shared reading • **4.I.1** demonstrate English comprehension by employing basic reading skills • **4.J** demonstrate English comprehension and expand reading skills by employing inferential skills and finding supporting text evidence **ELAR TEKS** • **G1.RC-1.D.1** make inferences about text
94	Think and Respond **Talk About It** **Write About It**	**ELPS** • **1.E.3, 4** internalize new academic language by using and reusing it in meaningful ways in speaking and writing activities that build concept and language attainment • **1.H** develop and expand repertoire of learning strategies • **2.H.1** understand implicit ideas in increasingly complex spoken language • **3.D.2** speak using content area vocabulary in context to build academic language proficiency • **4.1.2** expand reading skills • **4.F.7** use support from peers and teachers to enhance and confirm understanding • **4.G.3** demonstrate comprehension of increasingly complex English by responding to questions • **4.K** demonstrate English comprehension and expand reading skills by employing analytical skills such as evaluating written information and performing critical analysis • **5.B.2** write using content-based grade-level vocabulary **ELAR TEKS** • **G1.14.B** identify important facts and details in text, heard or read • **G1.14.D.1** use text features to locate specific information in text • **G1.15.A.1** follow written multi-step directions with picture cues to assist with understanding • **G1.RC-1.D.1** make inferences about text

95	Reread and Explain **Find Cause and Effect**	**ELPS** • **3.H.3** explain with increasing specificity and detail as more English is acquired • **4.I..2** expand reading skills • **4.F.8** use support from peers and teachers to develop vocabulary needed to comprehend increasingly challenging language
96	Word Work **Compound Words**	**ELPS** • **4.F.3** use visual and contextual support to develop vocabulary needed to comprehend increasingly challenging language **ELAR TEKS** • **G1.6.B.1** determine the meaning of compound words using knowledge of the meaning of their individual component words
102	Respond and Extend **Characters' Actions** **Talk Together**	**ELPS** • **2.G.1** understand the general meaning of spoken language ranging from situations in which topics are familiar to unfamiliar • **2.I.3** demonstrate listening comprehension of increasingly complex spoken English by responding to questions and requests • **4.F.8** use support from peers and teachers to develop vocabulary needed to comprehend increasingly challenging language • **4.K** demonstrate English comprehension and expand reading skills by employing analytical skills such as evaluating written information and performing critical analysis **ELAR TEKS** • **G1.9.B.2** describe reasons for [characters'] actions
103	Grammar and Spelling **Sentence Types**	**ELPS** • **3.C.2** speak using a variety of sentence lengths with increasing accuracy and ease • **3.C.3** speak using a variety of sentence types with increasing accuracy and ease • **4.F.4** use visual and contextual support to develop grasp of language structures needed to comprehend increasingly challenging language **ELAR TEKS** • **G1.21.C** recognize and use punctuation marks at the end of declarative, exclamatory, and interrogative sentences
104	Language **Express Ideas**	**ELPS** • **1.F.** use accessible language and learn new and essential language in the process • **2.E.3** use linguistic support to enhance and confirm understanding of increasingly complex and elaborated spoken language • **2.F.2** listen to and derive meaning from a variety of media to build and reinforce language attainment • **3.G.2** express ideas on a variety of social and grade-appropriate academic topics • **4.F.4** use visual and contextual support to develop grasp of language structures needed to comprehend increasingly challenging language
105, 107	Science Vocabulary Academic Vocabulary **Key Words** **Talk Together**	**ELPS** • **3.D.1** speak using content area vocabulary in context to internalize new English words • **3.G.2** express ideas on a variety of social and grade-appropriate academic topics • **4.F.3** use visual and contextual support to develop vocabulary needed to comprehend increasingly challenging language • **4.F 8, 9, 10** use support from peers and teachers to develop vocabulary, grasp of language structures, and background knowledge needed to comprehend increasingly challenging language **ELAR TEKS** • **G1.6.C.1** determine what words mean from how they are used in a sentence, either heard or read • **G1.28.A.2** share ideas about the topic under discussion, speaking clearly at an appropriate pace, using the conventions of language
106	Thinking Map **Classify Details** **Talk Together**	**ELPS** • **2.E.1, 2** use visual and contextual support support to enhance and confirm understanding of increasingly complex and elaborated spoken language • **2.G.2, 5, 8** understand the general meaning, main points, and details of spoken language ranging from situations in which language is familiar to unfamiliar • **4.D.1** use prereading supports to enhance comprehension of written text
A Year for Kiko		
108– 125	**Genre:** Realistic Fiction **Sensory Details** **Reading Strategy: Make Inferences**	**ELPS** • **4.F.6** use support from peers and teachers to read grade-level appropriate content area text • **4.G.1** demonstrate comprehension of increasingly complex English by participating in shared reading • **4.I.1** demonstrate English comprehension by employing basic reading skills • **4.J** demonstrate English comprehension and expand reading skills by employing inferential skills and finding supporting text evidence **ELAR TEKS** • **G1.11.A.1** recognize sensory details in literary text • **G1.RC-1.D.1** make inferences about text

UNIT 6	Up in the Air, *continued*	
126	Think and Respond **Talk About It** **Write About It**	**ELPS** • **1.E.3, 4** internalize new academic language by using and reusing it in meaningful ways in speaking and writing activities that build concept and language attainment • **1.H** develop and expand repertoire of learning strategies • **2.H.1** understand implicit ideas in increasingly complex spoken language commensurate with grade-level learning expectations • **3.D.2** speak using content area vocabulary in context to build academic language proficiency • **4.F.7** use support from peers and teachers to enhance and confirm understanding • **4.G.3** demonstrate comprehension of increasingly complex English by responding to questions • **4.K** demonstrate English comprehension and expand reading skills by employing analytical skills • **4.I.2** expand reading skills • **5.B.2** write using content-based grade-level vocabulary **ELAR TEKS** • **G1.4.B.3, 4** locate facts and details about stories • **G1.9.B.2, 3** describe reasons for [characters'] actions and feelings • **G1.11.A.1** recognize sensory details in literary text • **G1.RC-1.D.1** make inferences about text
127	Reread and Retell **Classify Details**	**ELPS** • **2.I.2** demonstrate listening comprehension of increasingly complex spoken English by retelling or summarizing spoken messages • **3.B.2** expand and internalize initial vocabulary by retelling simple stories and basic information represented or supported by pictures • **4.I.2** expand reading skills **ELAR TEKS** • **G1.4.B.4** locate details about stories
128	Word Work **Compound Words**	**ELPS** • **4.F.3** use visual and contextual support to develop vocabulary needed to comprehend increasingly challenging language **ELAR TEKS** • **G1.6.B.1** determine the meaning of compound words using knowledge of the meaning of their individual component words
132	Respond and Extend **Compare Genres** **Talk Together**	**ELPS** • **2.G.1** understand the general meaning of spoken language ranging from situations in which topics are familiar to unfamiliar • **4.F.8** use support from peers and teachers to develop vocabulary needed to comprehend increasingly challenging language • **4.K** demonstrate English comprehension and expand reading skills by employing analytical skills
133	Grammar **Ask Questions**	**ELPS** • **3.C.2** speak using a variety of sentence lengths with increasing accuracy and ease • **3.C.3** speak using a variety of sentence types with increasing accuracy and ease • **4.F.4** use visual and contextual support to develop grasp of language structures needed to comprehend increasingly challenging language **ELAR TEKS** • **G1.20.C.1** ask questions with appropriate subject-verb inversion • **G1.21.C.3, 6** recognize and use punctuation marks at the end of interrogative sentences
134–135	Writing Project **Write Like a Reporter (Write a Nonfiction Paragraph)** **Plan and Write**	**ELPS** • **1.G.** demonstrate an increasing ability to distinguish between, and knowledge of when to use, formal and informal English • **3.H.3** explain with increasing specificity and detail as more English is acquired **ELAR TEKS** • **G1.17.A.1** plan a first draft by generating ideas for writing • **G1.17.B.1** develop drafts by sequencing ideas through writing sentences • **G1.19.A.1** write brief compositions about topics of interest to the student
134–135	Writing Project continued **Write Like a Reporter (Write a Nonfiction Paragraph)** **Check Your Work**	**ELPS** • **5.C.1, 2** spell familiar English words and employ English spelling rules with increasing accuracy • **5.E.1** employ increasingly complex grammatical structures in content area writing **ELAR TEKS** • **G1.17.C.** revise drafts by adding or deleting a word, phrase, or sentence • **G1.17.D.** edit drafts for grammar, punctuation, and spelling using a teacher-developed rubric
134–135	Writing Project continued **Write Like a Reporter (Write a Nonfiction Paragraph)** **Finish and Share**	**ELPS** • **3.E.1** share information in cooperative learning interactions • **3.I.** adapt spoken language appropriately for formal and informal purposes **ELAR TEKS** • **G1.17.E** publish and share writing with others

136–137	Share Your Ideas	**ELPS** • **2.I.** 4 demonstrate listening comprehension of increasingly complex spoken English by collaborating with peers commensurate with content and grade-level needs • **3.E.1** share information in cooperative learning interactions • **3.I** adapt spoken language appropriately for formal and informal purposes • **5.B.1** write using newly acquired basic vocabulary **ELAR TEKS** • **G1.28.A.1** share information about the topic under discussion, speaking clearly at an appropriate pace, using the conventions of language • **G1.28.A.2** share ideas about the topic under discussion, speaking clearly at an appropriate pace, using the conventions of language

English Language Proficiency Standards (ELPS) English Language Arts and Reading (ELAR) TEKS, *continued*

UNIT 7 Then and Now		
138–139	Unit Opener **Share What You Know** **Build Background Video**	**ELPS** • **1.A.** use prior knowledge and experiences to understand meanings in English • **4.F.5** use visual and contextual support to develop background knowledge needed to comprehend increasingly challenging language **ELAR TEKS** • **G1.16.A.1** recognize different purposes of media (with adult assistance) • **G1.27.B.1** follow instructions that involve a short related sequence of actions
140	Language **Express Opinions**	**ELPS** • **1.F.** use accessible language and learn new and essential language in the process • **2.C.1** learn new language structures heard during classroom instruction and interactions • **2.E.3** use linguistic support to enhance and confirm understanding of increasingly complex and elaborated spoken language • **2.F.2** listen to and derive meaning from a variety of media to build and reinforce language attainment • **3.G.1** express opinions on a variety of social and grade-appropriate academic topics • **4.F.4** use visual and contextual support to develop grasp of language structures needed to comprehend increasingly challenging language
141, 143	Social Studies Vocabulary Academic Vocabulary **Key Words** **Talk Together**	**ELPS** • **3.D.** speak using content area vocabulary in context to internalize new English words and build academic language proficiency • **3.G.1** express opinions on a variety of social and grade-appropriate academic topics • **4.F.3** use visual and contextual support to develop vocabulary needed to comprehend increasingly challenging language • **4.F.8, 9, 10** use support from peers and teachers to develop vocabulary, grasp of language structures, and background knowledge needed to comprehend increasingly challenging language **ELAR TEKS** • **G1.6.C.1** determine what words mean from how they are used in a sentence, either heard or read • **G1.28.A.2** share ideas about the topic under discussion, speaking clearly at an appropriate pace, using the conventions of language
142	Thinking Map **Identify Main Idea and Details** **Talk Together**	**ELPS** • **2.E.1, 2** use visual and contextual support support to enhance and confirm understanding of increasingly complex and elaborated spoken language • **2.G.1** understand the general meaning of spoken language ranging from situations in which topics are familiar to unfamiliar • **2.G.3, 6, 9** understand the general meaning, main points, and details of spoken language ranging from situations in which contexts are familiar to unfamiliar • **4.D.1** use prereading supports to enhance comprehension of written text
Communication Then and Now		
144–161	**Genre:** History Article **Time Line** **Reading Strategy:** Visualize	**ELPS** • **4.F.6** use support from peers and teachers to read grade-level appropriate content area text • **4.G.1** demonstrate comprehension of increasingly complex English by participating in shared reading • **4.I.1** demonstrate English comprehension by employing basic reading skills
162	Think and Respond **Talk About It** **Write About It**	**ELPS** • **1.E.3, 4** internalize new academic language by using and reusing it in meaningful ways in speaking and writing activities that build concept and language attainment • **1.H** develop and expand repertoire of learning strategies • **2.H.1** understand implicit ideas in increasingly complex spoken language commensurate with grade-level learning expectations • **3.D.2** speak using content area vocabulary in context to build academic language proficiency • **3.G.1** express opinions on a variety of social and grade-appropriate academic topics • **4.1.2** expand reading skills • **4.F.7** use support from peers and teachers to enhance and confirm understanding • **4.G.3** demonstrate comprehension of increasingly complex English by responding to questions • **4.K** demonstrate English comprehension and expand reading skills by employing analytical skills such as evaluating written information and performing critical analysis • **5.B.2** write using content-based grade-level vocabulary **ELAR TEKS** • **G1.4.B.8** locate details about other texts • **G1.14.B.2** identify important details in text, heard or read • **G1.RC-1.F.1** make connections to own experiences
163	Reread and Summarize **Identify Main Idea and Details**	**ELPS** • **4.G.2** demonstrate comprehension of increasingly complex English by retelling or summarizing material • **4.I.2** expand reading skills **ELAR TEKS** • **G1.14.B** identify important facts and details in text, heard or read

UNIT 7 Then and Now, *continued*

Page	Lesson	Standards
164	Word Work **Alphabetize and Use a Dictionary**	**ELPS** • **4.F.3** use visual and contextual support to develop vocabulary needed to comprehend increasingly challenging language **ELAR TEKS** • **G1.6.E.1** alphabetize a series of words to the first letter • **G1.6.E.3** use a dictionary to find words
170	Respond and Extend **Compare Genres** **Talk Together**	**ELPS** • **2.G.1** understand the general meaning of spoken language ranging from situations in which topics are familiar to unfamiliar • **4.G.4** demonstrate comprehension of increasingly complex English by taking notes • **4.K** demonstrate English comprehension and expand reading skills by employing analytical skills such as evaluating written information and performing critical analysis **ELAR TEKS** • **G1.16.A.1** recognize different purposes of media (with adult assistance) • **G1.16.B.2** identify techniques used in media
171	Grammar and Spelling **Past Tense Verbs**	**ELPS** • **3.C.1** speak using a variety of grammatical structures with increasing accuracy and ease • **4.F.4** use visual and contextual support to develop grasp of language structures needed to comprehend increasingly challenging language • **5.E.1** employ increasingly complex grammatical structures in content area writing • **5.C.2** employ English spelling patterns with increasing accuracy • **5.C.3** employ English spelling rules with increasing accuracy **ELAR TEKS** • **G1.20.A.1.i** understand and use verbs (past) in the context of reading, writing, and speaking
172	Language **Express Feelings**	**ELPS** • **1.F.** use accessible language and learn new and essential language in the process • **2.E.3** use linguistic support to enhance and confirm understanding of increasingly complex and elaborated spoken language • **2.F.2** listen to and derive meaning from a variety of media to build and reinforce language attainment • **3.G.3** express feelings on a variety of social and grade-appropriate academic topics • **4.F.4** use visual and contextual support to develop grasp of language structures needed to comprehend increasingly challenging language
173, 175	Social Studies Vocabulary Academic Vocabulary **Key Words** **Talk Together**	**ELPS** • **2.G.1** understand the general meaning of spoken language ranging from situations in which topics are familiar to unfamiliar • **3.D.1** speak using content area vocabulary in context to internalize new English words • **3.G.3** express feelings on a variety of social and grade-appropriate academic topics • **4.F 3, 8, 9, 10** use visual and contextual support, support from peers and teachers to develop vocabulary, grasp of language structures, and background knowledge needed to comprehend increasingly challenging language **ELAR TEKS** • **G1.6.C.1** determine what words mean from how they are used in a sentence, either heard or read • **G1.28.A.2** share ideas about the topic under discussion, speaking clearly at an appropriate pace, using the conventions of language
174	Thinking Map **Describe Characters' Feelings** **Talk Together**	**ELPS** • **2.E.1, 2** use visual and contextual support support to enhance and confirm understanding of increasingly complex and elaborated spoken language • **2.G.2, 5, 8** understand the general meaning, main points, and details of spoken language ranging from situations in which language is familiar to unfamiliar • **4.D.1** use prereading supports to enhance comprehension of written text
A New Old Tune		
176–189	**Genre:** Realistic Fiction **Characters' Feelings** **Reading Strategy:** Visualize	**ELPS** • **4.F.6** use support from peers and teachers to read grade-level appropriate content area text • **4.G.1** demonstrate comprehension of increasingly complex English by participating in shared reading • **4.I.1** demonstrate English comprehension by employing basic reading skills

English Language Proficiency Standards (ELPS) English Language Arts and Reading (ELAR) TEKS, *continued*

UNIT 7 Then and Now, *continued*		
190	Think and Respond **Talk About It** **Write About It**	**ELPS** • **1.E.3, 4** internalize new academic language by using and reusing it in meaningful ways in speaking and writing activities that build concept and language attainment • **1.H** develop and expand repertoire of learning strategies • **2.H.1** understand implicit ideas in increasingly complex spoken language commensurate with grade-level learning expectations • **3.D.2** speak using content area vocabulary in context to build academic language proficiency • **4.F.7** use support from peers and teachers to enhance and confirm understanding • **4.G.3** demonstrate comprehension of increasingly complex English by responding to questions • **4.K** demonstrate English comprehension and expand reading skills by employing analytical skills • **4.I.2** expand reading skills • **5.B.2** write using content-based grade-level vocabulary **ELAR TEKS** • **G1.9.B.2** describe reasons for [characters'] actions and feelings • **G1.RC-1.D.1** make inferences about text • **G1.RC-1.F.1** make connections to own experiences
191	Reread and Retell **Describe Character's Feelings**	**ELPS** • **2.I.2** demonstrate listening comprehension of increasingly complex spoken English by retelling or summarizing spoken messages • **3.B.2** expand and internalize initial vocabulary by retelling simple stories and basic information represented or supported by pictures • **4.I.2** expand reading skills **ELAR TEKS** • **G1.9.B.1, 3** describe characters in a story and reasons for [characters'] feelings
192	Word Work **Alphabetize and Use a Dictionary**	**ELPS** • **4.F.3** use visual and contextual support to develop vocabulary needed to comprehend increasingly challenging language **ELAR TEKS** • **G1.6.E.2** alphabetize a series of words to the second letter • **G1.6.E.3** use a dictionary to find words • **G1.22.E.1** use resources to find correct spellings
198	Respond and Extend **Compare Genres** **Talk Together**	**ELPS** • **2.G.1** understand the general meaning of spoken language ranging from situations in which topics are familiar to unfamiliar • **4.K** demonstrate English comprehension and expand reading skills by employing analytical skills
199	Grammar **Future Tense Verbs**	**ELPS** • **3.C.4** speak using a variety of connecting words with increasing accuracy and ease. • **4.F.4** use visual and contextual support to develop grasp of language structures needed to comprehend increasingly challenging language • **5.E.1** employ increasingly complex grammatical structures in content area writing **ELAR TEKS** • **G1.20.A.1.iii** understand and use verbs (future) in the context of reading, writing, and speaking
200–201	Writing Project **Write as a Friend (Write a Friendly Letter)** **Plan and Write**	**ELPS** • **1.G.** demonstrate an increasing ability to distinguish between, and knowledge of when to use, formal and informal English • **3.G.1** express opinions on a variety of social and grade-appropriate academic topics **ELAR TEKS** • **G1.17.A.1** plan a first draft by generating ideas for writing • **G1.17.B.1** develop drafts by sequencing ideas through writing sentences • **G1.19.B.** write short letters that put ideas in a chronological sequence, put ideas in a logical sequence, and use appropriate conventions
200	Writing Project continued **Write as a Friend (Write a Friendly Letter)** **Check Your Work**	**ELPS** • **5.C.1, 2** spell familiar English words and employ English spelling rules with increasing accuracy • **5.D.3** edit writing for standard grammar and usage, including appropriate verb tenses • **5.F.1** write using a variety of grade-appropriate sentence lengths in increasingly accurate way **ELAR TEKS** • **G1.17.C.** revise drafts by adding or deleting a word, phrase, or sentence • **G1.17.D.** edit drafts for grammar, punctuation, and spelling using a teacher-developed rubric
200–201	Writing Project continued **Write as a Friend (Write a Friendly Letter)** **Finish and Share**	**ELPS** • **3.E.1** share information in cooperative learning interactions • **3.I.** adapt spoken language appropriately for formal and informal purposes **ELAR TEKS** • **G1.17.E** publish and share writing with others

Pages	Lesson	Standards
202–203	Share Your Ideas	**ELPS** • **2.I.** 4 demonstrate listening comprehension of increasingly complex spoken English by collaborating with peers commensurate with content and grade-level needs • **3.E.1** share information in cooperative learning interactions • **3.F.1** ask [for] information ranging from concrete vocabulary to abstract and content-based vocabulary • **3.I** adapt spoken language appropriately for formal and informal purposes **ELAR TEKS** • **G1.6.E.1** alphabetize a series of words to the first letter • **G1.6.E.2** alphabetize a series of words to the second letter • **G1.28.A.1** share information about the topic under discussion, speaking clearly at an appropriate pace, using the conventions of language • **G1.28.A.2** share ideas about the topic under discussion, speaking clearly at an appropriate pace, using the conventions of language

English Language Proficiency Standards (ELPS) English Language Arts and Reading (ELAR) TEKS, *continued*

UNIT 8 Get Out the Map!		
204–205	Unit Opener **Share What You Know** **Build Background Video**	**ELPS** • **1.A.** use prior knowledge and experiences to understand meanings in English • **4.F.5** use visual and contextual support to develop background knowledge needed to comprehend increasingly challenging language **ELAR TEKS** • **G1.16.A.1** recognize different purposes of media (with adult assistance) • **G1.27.B.1** follow instructions that involve a short related sequence of actions • **G1.27.B.3** give oral instructions that involve a short related sequence of actions
206	Language **Follow Directions**	**ELPS** • **1.F.** use accessible language and learn new and essential language in the process • **2.E.3** use linguistic support to enhance and confirm understanding of increasingly complex and elaborated spoken language • **2.F.2** listen to and derive meaning from a variety of media to build and reinforce language attainment • **3.B.3** expand and internalize initial English vocabulary by learning and using routine language needed for classroom communication • **4.F.4** use visual and contextual support to develop grasp of language structures needed to comprehend increasingly challenging language
207, 209	Social Studies Vocabulary Academic Vocabulary **Key Words** **Talk Together**	**ELPS** • **3.D.** speak using content area vocabulary in context to internalize new English words and build academic language proficiency • **4.F.3** use visual and contextual support to develop vocabulary needed to comprehend increasingly challenging language • **4.F 8, 9, 10** use support from peers and teachers to develop vocabulary, grasp of language structures, and background knowledge needed to comprehend increasingly challenging language **ELAR TEKS** • **G1.6.C.1** determine what words mean from how they are used in a sentence, either heard or read • **G1.28.A.2** share ideas about the topic under discussion, speaking clearly at an appropriate pace, using the conventions of language
208	Thinking Map **Use Information** **Talk Together**	**ELPS** • **2.E.1, 2** use visual and contextual support support to enhance and confirm understanding of increasingly complex and elaborated spoken language • **2.G.2, 5, 8** understand the general meaning, main points, and details of spoken language ranging from situations in which language is familiar to unfamiliar • **4.D.1** use prereading supports to enhance comprehension of written text **ELAR TEKS** • **G1.15.B.1** explain the meaning of specific signs • **G1.15.B.2** explain the meaning of specific symbols
If Maps Could Talk		
210–223	**Genre:** Informational Text **Maps**	**ELPS** • **4.F.6** use support from peers and teachers to read grade-level appropriate content area text • **4.G.1** demonstrate comprehension of increasingly complex English by participating in shared reading • **4.I.1** demonstrate English comprehension by employing basic reading skills
224	Think and Respond **Talk About It** **Write About It**	**ELPS** • **1.E.3** internalize new academic language by using and reusing it in meaningful ways in speaking activities that build concept and language attainment • **1.E.4** internalize new academic language by using and reusing it in meaningful ways in writing activities that build concept and language attainment • **1.H** develop and expand repertoire of learning strategies • **3.D.2** speak using content area vocabulary in context to build academic language proficiency • **4.1.2** expand reading skills • **4.F.7** use support from peers and teachers to enhance and confirm understanding • **4.G.3** demonstrate comprehension of increasingly complex English by responding to questions • **4.K** demonstrate English comprehension and expand reading skills by employing analytical skills such as evaluating written information and performing critical analysis • **5.B.2** write using content-based grade-level vocabulary **ELAR TEKS** • **G1.14.B** identify important facts and details in text, heard or read • **G1.14.D.1** use text features to locate specific information in text • **G1.19.C.2** write brief comments on informational texts

Page	Lesson	Standards
225	Reread and Retell **Use Information**	**ELPS** • **2.I.2** demonstrate listening comprehension of increasingly complex spoken English by retelling or summarizing spoken messages • **3.B.2** expand and internalize initial vocabulary by retelling basic information represented or supported by pictures • **4.I.2** expand reading skills **ELAR TEKS** • **G1.14.C** retell the order of events in a text by referring to the words and illustrations
226	Word Work **Suffixes**	**ELPS** • **4.F.3** use visual and contextual support to develop vocabulary needed to comprehend increasingly challenging language
230	Respond and Extend **Compare Genres** **Talk Together**	**ELPS** • **2.G.1** understand the general meaning of spoken language ranging from situations in which topics are familiar to unfamiliar • **4.K** demonstrate English comprehension and expand reading skills by employing analytical skills such as evaluating written information and performing critical analysis
231	Grammar and Spelling **Adverbs**	**ELPS** • **3.C.4** speak using a variety of connecting words with increasing accuracy and ease. • **4.F.4** use visual and contextual support to develop grasp of language structures needed to comprehend increasingly challenging language • **5.C.2** employ English spelling patterns with increasing accuracy • **5.C.3** employ English spelling rules with increasing accuracy **ELAR TEKS** • **G1.20.A.4** understand and use adverbs in the context of reading, writing, and speaking
232	Language **Tell a Story**	**ELPS** • **1.F.** use accessible language and learn new and essential language in the process • **2.E.3** use linguistic support to enhance and confirm understanding of increasingly complex and elaborated spoken language • **2.F.2** listen to and derive meaning from a variety of media to build and reinforce language attainment • **3.H.1** narrate with increasing specificity and detail as more English is acquired • **4.F.4** use visual and contextual support to develop grasp of language structures needed to comprehend increasingly challenging language
233, 235	Social Studies Vocabulary Academic Vocabulary **Key Words** **Talk Together**	**ELPS** • **3.D.1** speak using content area vocabulary in context to internalize new English words • **4.F.3** use visual and contextual support to develop vocabulary needed to comprehend increasingly challenging language • **4.F 8, 9, 10** use support from peers and teachers to develop vocabulary, grasp of language structures, and background knowledge needed to comprehend increasingly challenging language **ELAR TEKS** • **G1.6.C.1** determine what words mean from how they are used in a sentence, either heard or read • **G1.28.A.2** share ideas about the topic under discussion, speaking clearly at an appropriate pace, using the conventions of language
234	Thinking Map **Identify Problem and Solution** **Talk Together**	**ELPS** • **2.E.1, 2** use visual and contextual support support to enhance and confirm understanding of increasingly complex and elaborated spoken language • **2.G.2, 5, 8** understand the general meaning, main points, and details of spoken language ranging from situations in which language is familiar to unfamiliar • **4.D.1** use prereading supports to enhance comprehension of written text
Caperucita Roja		
236–257	**Genre:** Modern Fairy Tale **Recurring Phrases**	**ELPS** • **4.F.6** use support from peers and teachers to read grade-level appropriate content area text • **4.G.1** demonstrate comprehension of increasingly complex English by participating in shared reading • **4.I.1** demonstrate English comprehension by employing basic reading skills **ELAR TEKS** • **G1.7.B.2** explain the function of recurring phrases in traditional fairy tales

English Language Proficiency Standards (ELPS) English Language Arts and Reading (ELAR) TEKS, *continued*

UNIT 8	Get Out the Map!, *continued*	
258	Think and Respond **Talk About It** **Write About It**	**ELPS** • **1.E.3, 4** internalize new academic language by using and reusing it in meaningful ways in speaking and writing activities that build concept and language attainment • **1.H** develop and expand repertoire of learning strategies • **3.D.2** speak using content area vocabulary in context to build academic language proficiency • **4.F.7** use support from peers and teachers to enhance and confirm understanding • **4.G.3** demonstrate comprehension of increasingly complex English by responding to questions • **4.K** demonstrate English comprehension and expand reading skills by employing analytical skills • **4.I.2** expand reading skills • **5.B.2** write using content-based grade-level vocabulary **ELAR TEKS** • **G1.4.B.4** locate details about stories • **G1.7.A.1** connect the meaning of a well-known story to personal experiences
259	Reread and Retell **Identify Problem and Solution**	**ELPS** • **2.I.2** demonstrate listening comprehension of increasingly complex spoken English by retelling or summarizing spoken messages • **3.B.2** expand and internalize initial vocabulary by retelling simple stories and basic information represented or supported by pictures • **4.I.2** expand reading skills **ELAR TEKS** • **G1.9.A.1** describe the plot (problem and solution) • **G1.9.A.2** retell a story's beginning, middle, and end with attention to the sequence of events
260	Word Work **Prefixes**	**ELPS** • **4.F.3** use visual and contextual support to develop vocabulary needed to comprehend increasingly challenging language
266	Respond and Extend **Compare Genres** **Talk Together**	**ELPS** • **2.G.1** understand the general meaning of spoken language ranging from situations in which topics are familiar to unfamiliar • **4.K** demonstrate English comprehension and expand reading skills by employing analytical skills **ELAR TEKS** • **G1.10.A.** determine whether a story is true or a fantasy and explain why
267	Grammar and Spelling **Prepositions**	**ELPS** • **3.C.4** speak using a variety of connecting words with increasing accuracy and ease. • **4.F.4** use visual and contextual support to develop grasp of language structures needed to comprehend increasingly challenging language • **5.C.2, 3** employ English spelling patterns and rules with increasing accuracy **ELAR TEKS** • **G1.20.A.5** understand and use prepositions and prepositional phrases in the context of reading, writing, and speaking
268–269	Writing Project **Write as a Reader (Write a Literary Response)** **Plan and Write**	**ELPS** • **1.G.** demonstrate an increasing ability to distinguish between, and knowledge of when to use, formal and informal English **ELAR TEKS** • **G1.17.A.1** plan a first draft by generating ideas for writing • **G1.17.B.1** develop drafts by sequencing ideas through writing sentences • **G1.19.C.1** write brief comments on literary texts
268–269	Writing Project continued **Write as a Reader (Write a Literary Response)** **Check Your Work**	**ELPS** • **5.C.1, 2** spell familiar English words and employ English spelling rules with increasing accuracy • **5.E.1** employ increasingly complex grammatical structures in content area writing • **5.F.2** write using a variety of grade-appropriate sentence patterns in increasingly accurate ways **ELAR TEKS** • **G1.17.C.** revise drafts by adding or deleting a word, phrase, or sentence • **G1.17.D.** edit drafts for grammar, punctuation, and spelling using a teacher-developed rubric
268–269	Writing Project continued **Write as a Reader (Write a Literary Response)** **Finish and Share**	**ELPS** • **3.E.1** share information in cooperative learning interactions • **3.I.** adapt spoken language appropriately for formal and informal purposes **ELAR TEKS** • **G1.17.E** publish and share writing with others

270–271	Share Your Ideas	**ELPS** • **2.H.2** understand information in increasingly complex spoken language commensurate with grade-level learning expectations • **2.I.1** demonstrate listening comprehension of increasingly complex spoken English by following directions • **2.I.4** demonstrate listening comprehension of increasingly complex spoken English by collaborating with peers commensurate with content and grade-level needs • **3.E.1** share information in cooperative learning interactions • **3.I** adapt spoken language appropriately for formal and informal purposes **ELAR TEKS** • **G1.15.B.2** explain the meaning of specific symbols • **G1.28.A.1** share information about the topic under discussion, speaking clearly at an appropriate pace, using the conventions of language • **G1.28.A.2** share ideas about the topic under discussion, speaking clearly at an appropriate pace, using the conventions of language

Grade 1, Volume 2, Content Standards		
Unit 5 Creature Features		
page 2	Science	• **S.G1.10.A.i** investigate how the external characteristics of an animal are related to where it lives • **S.G1.10.A.ii** investigate how the external characteristics of an animal are related to how it moves • **S.G1.10.A.iii** investigate how the external characteristics of an animal are related to what it eats
Unit 6 Up in the Air		
page 70	Science	• **S.G1.8.C.i** identify characteristics of the seasons of the year • **S.G1.8.D.i** demonstrate that air is all around us • **S.G1.8.D.ii** observe that wind is moving air
Unit 7 Past and Present		
page 138	Social Studies	• **SS.G1.3.A** distinguish among past, present, and future • **SS.G1.3.B** create a calendar or timeline • **SS.G1.3.C.i** use vocabulary related to chronology, including yesterday • **SS.G1.3.C.ii** use vocabulary related to chronology, including today • **SS.G1.3.C.iii** use vocabulary related to chronology, including tomorrow • **SS.G1.16.A** describe how household tools and appliances have changed the ways families live • **SS.G1.16.B.i** describe how technology has changed communication • **SS.G1.16.B.ii** describe how technology has changed transportation • **SS.G1.16.B.iii** describe how technology has changed recreation • **SS.G1.16.C** describe how technology has changed the way people work
Unit 8 Get Out the Map!		
page 204	Social Studies	• **SS.G1.4.A** locate places using the four cardinal directions • **SS.G1.5.A.ii** create simple maps to identify the location of places in the school • **SS.G1.5.A.iii** create simple maps to identify the location of places in the community and beyond • **SS.G1.5.A.v** use simple maps to identify the location of places in the school • **SS.G1.5.A.vi** use simple maps to identify the location of places in the community and beyond • **SS.G1.5.B.i** locate places of significance on maps

For additional coverage of the English Language Proficiency Standards (ELPS) and Texas Essential Knowledge and Skills (TEKS), use these companion programs:

Reach into Phonics

Grade 1 Literature Big Books